Debating Sex
and Gender

Debating Sex and Gender

GEORGIA WARNKE
University of California, Riverside

New York   Oxford
OXFORD UNIVERSITY PRESS
2011

Oxford University Press, Inc., publishes works that further Oxford University's objective of excellence in research, scholarship, and education.

Oxford   New York
Auckland   Cape Town   Dar es Salaam   Hong Kong   Karachi
Kuala Lumpur   Madrid   Melbourne   Mexico City   Nairobi
New Delhi   Shanghai   Taipei   Toronto

With offices in
Argentina   Austria   Brazil   Chile   Czech Republic   France   Greece
Guatemala   Hungary   Italy   Japan   Poland   Portugal   Singapore
South Korea   Switzerland   Thailand   Turkey   Ukraine   Vietnam

Published by Oxford University Press, Inc.
198 Madison Avenue, New York, New York 10016
http://www.oup.com

Library of Congress Cataloging-in-Publication Data
Warnke, Georgia.
  Debating sex and gender / by Georgia Warnke.
    p. cm.—(Fundamentals of philosophy series)
Includes bibliographical references and index.
ISBN: 978-0-19-530885-3
1. Identity (Psychology).   2. Sex differences.   3. Identity (Psychology)—Social aspects.
4. Ethnicity.   I. Title.
BF697.W323   2010
305.301—dc22   2010018243

Printing number: 9 8 7 6 5 4 3

Printed in the United States of America
on acid-free paper

CONTENTS

PREFACE

This book is an introduction to contemporary feminist thought that tries to be clear without sacrificing the ability to demonstrate the depth and richness of that thought. The concepts of sex and gender may seem simple: *Sex* refers to physical and biological characteristics of male and female human beings, while *gender* refers to varying social, political, and cultural norms that various communities attach to these characteristics. Yet, as it turns out, neither term is at all straightforward. Instead, once we start to investigate what sex is meant to be, what gender is meant to be, and what their relations both to each other and to other aspects of our identities are meant to be, we find ourselves following a thread that takes us deep into some of the most interesting theories and theorists in modern philosophy and political theory.

Four sets of debates and discussions will serve as landmarks to help guide us in this tour:

1. *The debates over the relation between sex and gender.* Does sex causes gender, so feminists were wrong to think they could distinguish them? Conversely, does gender so thoroughly cause sex that sex is, in fact, nothing but gender? Or do gender and sex actually have no relation to one another, so we can mix and match them in any way we desire?
2. *The discussions of quantity.* Whatever the relation between sex and gender, how many of each are there, actually? Should we assume that there are at most two sexes and at most two genders? And how many different ways can sex and gender be related to one another?
3. *The debates over the idea, associated with the work of Judith Butler, of gender as a performative.* What is the relevance of ideas of gender as a performance to ideas of gender as a performative? What critical and emancipatory potential does the latter idea have, if any?

4. *The debates over the intersection of gender with race, class, and host of other characteristics of identity.* If we acknowledge that one's gender identity is inextricably linked with one's racial identity, class identity, and so on, is there anything left to gender at all?

Each of the first four chapters of this book deals with one of these sets. The fifth chapter tries to resolve at least some of the debates by situating sex and/or gender within a broader theory of identity. But whatever the outcome of that attempt, the conclusion of the book is clear: Feminist philosophy and political theory are among the most dynamic areas in contemporary thought and certainly repay thorough study.

I would like to thank John Fischer at University of California, Riverside for inviting me to try my hand at writing for his *Fundamentals of Philosophy* series. I would also especially like to thank the four reviewers of the original manuscript of this book: Thomas De Frantz at MIT, Leslie Jo Frasier at Indiana University, Nancy Tuana at Pennsylvania State University, and Melissa Wilcox at Whitman College. With the usual caveat that whatever failings the book retains are my own, I want to assure them that their extraordinarily helpful comments have improved the final product.

Debating Sex
and Gender

INTRODUCTION

Since at least the 1970s, many scholars and feminist theorists in the English-speaking world have distinguished between sex and gender. They use the term *sex* to designate the aspects of human biology that differ between male and female human beings. They use the term *gender* to refer to culturally and historically based differences in the roles, attitudes, and behaviors of men and women. Their point in distinguishing between sex and gender in this way is to allow a clear separation between the unchanging, material aspects of male and female bodies—one's sex—and the changing historical and cultural divisions of feminine and masculine functions and responsibilities—one's gender. For example, while it may be a fact of sexual biology that female human beings, not male ones, bear children, it is merely a matter of gender conventions that primarily women, not men, also rear them. Moreover, as a matter of convention, such gender roles and responsibilities can be changed. As Toril Moi explains, "Gender may be pictured as a barricade thrown up against the insidious pervasiveness of sex."[1] Distinguishing gender from sex eradicates the supposed biological foundation for differences in functions between men and women and embeds them firmly in history, culture, and society.

Almost as soon as feminists and women's studies scholars began to distinguish between sex and gender, however, they and their critics began to raise questions about both the distinction and the two terms that comprise it. This book is an introduction to some of these questions and to the debates that surround them. We start with the issue of whether gender really is separate from sex or whether, instead, the roles and functions we associate with gender actually grow out of biological differences. A myriad of experiments and investigations over the years have tried to decide this issue. What happens, for example, if you take identical twin male infants and try to raise one to possess the gender identity of a girl? Does it work,

1

thereby showing that social and cultural gender is independent of biological sex? Or does the girl's original sex override her upbringing? What happens if you are brought up as a girl but suddenly sprout a penis? Does your new sex cause you to change your gender? Suppose we take a thirty-year survey of math and science abilities in girls and boys. Will that allow us to decide whether biology or culture causes identifiable differences? And what if we can find other genders besides masculine and feminine ones or other sexes besides male and female ones?

As we follow various strands of the debate over the causal role of sex, we shall discover issues that do not seem to lend themselves to strictly empirical investigations. For instance, the distinction between sex and gender presupposes a natural, unchanging biological sex and a conventional, changing cultural gender. But what if sex itself is a product of culture and convention? Surely, we could use many body parts other than sexual organs to distinguish people: Why not distinguish between those with knobby knees and those without them, or between those with "innie" belly buttons and those with "outies"? Why should we use sexual organs instead of belly buttons as one of our most basic ways to distinguish people? Presumably, our reasons for doing so refer to distinctions necessary for the very reproduction of the species. Yet, even if these are sound reasons, they are surely *our* reasons and not somehow written into nature. So why should we call sex a part of nature and gender a part of culture? Is there really anything to our definitions other than social, historical, and culture purposes? Is there really anything to sex outside of gender?

These questions lead to another one: What, exactly, is gender? If it is not an outgrowth of or somehow connected to sex, what is it? We shall see that some feminists and women's studies scholars consider it an act or performance, some the result of women's mothering, some a moral tendency, and many a factor so bound up with race and class as to be nothing in itself at all. Try to point to that part of yourself that involves only your gender independently of your race, socioeconomic status, or even age. No matter how nice it would be to rescue some aspect of one's identity from one's advancing age, it is by no means clear that we can do so. Is the gender of a young woman who has little children and a husband the same as the gender of an older, postmenopausal woman? And suppose we add different races, nationalities, and classes into the mix. If we pursue reflections on the cultural constitution of sex and the intersections of gender, it as if gender swallows up sex and then itself disappears. Like the Cheshire Cat, gender leaves us with only a grin. We tried to use gender as a tool against sexism only to see it fade away, leaving women's studies scholars to worry that they have written themselves out of a job and feminists to wonder whether they have undermined the very basis of struggles for women's rights.

In Chapters Four and Five of this book, we explore some of the ways theorists try to rematerialize the Cheshire Cat. Nevertheless, we do not try to resolve all debates surrounding sex and gender or ferret out all of their permutations. Instead, we try to provide one guided tour through the terrain in order to give a sense of the rich resources to which feminists and women's studies scholars appeal. Reflections on sex and gender are notably interdisciplinary, making use of, at minimum, history, philosophy, sociology, anthropology, and the biological sciences. Philosophical resources alone include phenomenology, existentialism, philosophy of language, poststructuralism, and postmodernism. I presuppose no prior knowledge of these multiple fields in this book and do not propose to use this text to introduce them. To mention them here is only to suggest that we can start anywhere in the field of sex and gender studies and find a wealth of riches to mine. We begin with the terms *sex* and *gender* themselves.

CHAPTER ONE

Sex and Gender

In her influential 1975 essay "The Traffic in Women," Gayle Rubin argues that "[e]very society has a sex/gender system—a set of arrangements by which the biological raw material of human sex and procreation is shaped by human, social intervention and satisfied in a conventional manner."[1] As Rubin understands sex, then, it pertains to the "raw material" of the bodies of male and female human beings, while as she understands gender, it pertains to the roles and functions those human beings have in the societies and cultures of which they are a part. Rubin knows that these roles and functions vary extensively across different cultures. Nonetheless, she sees sexism as the general phenomenon by which human beings who are female according to their biology become "domesticated women," or workhorses for men, according to the various gender conventions that dictate specific roles and functions. Rubin denies that any natural laws can explain the move from sex, or female, to gender, or woman. She thinks certain facts of nature compose two distinct male and female sexes, but she insists that only historical and cultural conventions explain the gendered roles and functions these sexes possess. Biological differences in themselves thus bear no responsibility for the second-class status to which women have been relegated throughout most of history. If women are largely confined to the home and primarily responsible for the care of husbands and children, this situation, Rubin argues, is not a product of sex but, instead, of gender—not a result of nature but rather a result of history, culture, society, and most emphatically, of economics. The arrangements, she claims, under which the male sex assumes social, cultural, and economic entitlements while the female assumes social, cultural, and economic burdens are all purely conventional.

This distinction between an unchangeable biological sex and a changeable social gender is clear and simple. As a revived feminism began to take root in the 1970s—the theoretical and practical initiative often called "second wave feminism"—the distinction was also quite useful for highlighting the absence of any biological foundation either for unequal social and economic arrangements or for the traditional domestic roles and functions of women. Although most cultures and societies have thus far privileged men over women, Rubin and the feminists who follow her argue that cultures and societies need not do so. Rather, because women's traditional roles and functions hamper their development, restrict their freedom, and undermine equality, existing sex/gender systems, Rubin maintains, not only can but surely must be changed.

This attempt to distinguish sex and gender has given rise to an extensive debate and an on-going series of questions. We shall look at some of this discussion in this chapter, but we begin with two sources for the distinction as second wave feminism adopted it: Simone de Beauvoir's 1949 book in existential philosophy, *The Second Sex*,[2] and John Money and Anke Ehrhardt's 1972 book on the medical treatment of the intersexed and transsexuals, *Man and Woman, Boy and Girl*.[3]

THE SECOND SEX

Simone de Beauvoir does not herself use the terms sex and gender, and some feminist theorists think it is a mistake to impose the distinction retroactively on her book.[4] Still, the most famous sentence in *The Second Sex* is "One is not born, but rather becomes a woman,"[5] a sentence that at the very least suggests a distinction between a female sex with which one is born and a feminine gender that one acquires. Beauvoir also implies the distinction in the conundrum she raises at the beginning of her introduction: "All agree in recognizing the fact that females exist in the human species... And yet we are told that femininity is in danger; we are exhorted to be women, remain women, become women."[6] Femininity can be in danger, however, only if it is not an inevitable outgrowth of being born female—in other words, only if gender is not the same as sex. Likewise, female human beings can be exhorted to be, to remain, and to become women only if they have other options, only if they need not be, remain, or become women and, hence, only if there is a difference between being a female and being a woman. Being a woman—or in other words, possessing a feminine gender—is not a characteristic that comes with birth or with a female sex. Instead, it must be acquired, learned, and adopted. While a female human being's sex is "natural," Beauvoir implies, a woman's feminine gender is not. From where, then, does it come, or how do female human beings acquire it? In order to answer this question, *The Second Sex* surveys philosophy, anthropology, psychology, and history. We look at its analyses here only insofar as they contribute to the development of the distinction between sex and gender.

Beauvoir's description of female biological sex is certainly less than enthralled. She maintains that girls usually are relatively healthy until puberty, but she thinks that things go decidedly downhill after that. Witness, for instance, her description of menstruation: "Fever is frequent; pains in the abdomen are felt; often diarrhea is observed; frequently there are also swelling of the liver, retention of urea and albuminuria; many subjects have sore throat and difficulties with hearing and sight; perspiration is increased."[7] Menstruating is thus hardly for the faint of heart but pregnancy is even worse. Beauvoir calls it a "profound alienation," which brings with it such a severe loss of essential minerals that "all that a healthy and well-nourished woman can hope for is to recoup these losses without too much difficulty after childbirth." As for childbirth itself, Beauvoir calls this "painful and dangerous," and she claims that "[i]f the woman is not strong, repeated childbearing will make her prematurely old and misshapen." "Nursing is also a tiring service,"[8] she says, after which women can look forward to renewed menstruating and all of its ills. Only menopause brings an end to this "servitude"—if, to be sure, a woman makes it that far without first succumbing to death, "chlorosis, tuberculosis, scoliosis and osteomyeletis."[9] Yet, Beauvoir terms even menopause a "crisis." In sum, whereas a man's biological life "runs an even course, without crises and generally without mishap,"[10] a woman's biological life is filled with "crises of puberty and the menopause, monthly 'curse,' long and often difficult pregnancy, painful and sometimes dangerous childbirth, illnesses, unexpected symptoms and complications."[11]

Beauvoir suggests that a female's sexual biology has devastated her life prospects from human prehistory onwards. She writes of prehistoric man, "He burst out of the present, he opened the future…he has worked not merely to conserve the world as given; he has broken through its frontiers, he has laid down the foundation of a new future."[12] Alone among animals, Beauvoir asserts, male human beings have disdained simply to comply with the natural circumstances that might have been laid before them. Instead, they sought always to transform them. In their prehistory, they made tools to tame their environment, and after they had tamed it as well as they could with the tools they had, they created new tools and tamed it again, reharnessing it to do their bidding and to serve their interests. In Beauvoir's vocabulary, men thus transcended mere biological "Life" for a specifically human "Existence."[13] Beauvoir's philosophical foundations are in existentialism, a school of thought which, for her, entails that the meaning of human existence is neither given with human life nor bestowed upon it by God. The being of human beings possesses no intrinsic or otherworldly significance. Rather, human beings must create significance; they must give their life meaning by actively taking it up and intentionally crafting their own future. Rather than living a mere biological life as animals, reacting to circumstances as those circumstances present themselves, men thus engage in what Beauvoir calls projects—ventures that exceed simple acts of survival and create meaningful forms of existence that human beings can choose. Indeed, she argues, the fact of war shows that men are willing to risk their merely biological lives, proving "dramatically that life is not the supreme value for man."[14] This supreme value is instead a meaningful and specifically human existence.

Not so for prehistoric women. Beauvoir contrasts man's willingness to risk life with woman's function to give life. Likewise, she contrasts the intentional transformation of life into existence through projects with the passive, female activity of simply bearing and raising children. This life keeps a woman "closely bound to her body, like an animal," Beauvoir insists.[15] Unlike men, women are "the prey of the species."[16] In human prehistory, they did not take part in either transformative labor or life-transcending battle, and their absence set the trajectory for their entire future history. The functions of bearing, nursing, and weaning children are parts of an animal life, not parts of a free human existence. In tying themselves to these, women missed out on the "transcendence" of mere life through projects and bound themselves to what Beauvoir calls "immanence" within it.[17] In bearing and rearing children, they constructed no reason or meaning for their lives, no project such as invention or war that could go beyond mere survival. Instead, the childbearing and childrearing in which they ceaselessly engaged was substantially unchanging and repetitive, and because it was compatible with other forms of domestic work, these, too, fell to prehistoric women. "The clean becomes soiled, the soiled is made clean, over and over, day after day."[18] In such repetitive functions, Beauvoir writes, a "[w]oman found no reason for a lofty affirmation of her existence—she submitted passively to her biological fate,"[19] a fate that repeated itself in an identical way for centuries. Men transformed every new present toward a new future; women bred and fed and did so in no new or creative ways. As Beauvoir concludes, "In serving the species, the human male also remodels the face of the earth, he creates new instruments, he invents, he shapes the future." The "misfortune" of the human female, in contrast, "is to have been biologically destined for the repetition of Life, when even in her own view Life does not carry within itself its reasons for being, reason that are more important than the life itself."[20]

More recent anthropological research casts a good deal of doubt on Beauvoir's account of the activities of prehistoric women. For example, the research team of Kristin Hawkes, James F. O'Connell, and Nicholas G.

Blurton Jones conducted an extensive study of the Hadza people of northern Tanzania, who continue to live in ways that scientists think approximate the evolutionary situation. These researchers discovered that on average, adult Hadza men and adult Hadza women spend about the same amount of time on most activities. Hence, it is not at all clear that prehistoric women confined themselves to breeding and domestic chores. In fact, Hawkes, O'Connell, and Jones found that female "foraging" rather than male hunting supplied the Hadza families with most of their calories. [21]

Prehistoric women may also have helped shape a specifically human existence. One factor separating early human beings from other animals was the extended childhoods the former enjoyed, childhoods that gave the human brain time to develop. According to Sarah Blaffer Hrdy, what allowed for these extended childhoods was the help of those she calls "allomothers," older aunts and grandmothers who had gone through menopause and thus had no infants of their own for whom they needed to care. Hrdy calls this supposition "the grandmother's clock hypothesis." [22] If we ask why human females evolved to live past the end of their usefulness as reproductive machines, part of the answer may be that by doing so, they served to extend the period of childhood dependency. When the human mothers of toddlers gave birth to new babies, the toddlers did not need to fend for themselves, because their allomothers were available to tend to them. [23]

Despite this not insignificant contribution, Beauvoir would probably still not accord women's role in human intelligence the status of a project. In her view, raising children through a long period of dependency remains an "immanent" chore, mindlessly serving the reproduction of the species. But we might ask why. Why should it not constitute a project to establish the foundations on which one's children or grandchildren, or one's sister's children, can flourish? Why should doing so not lift one from life to existence as surely as hunting large animals lifts a man? Beauvoir does admit, "Cooking is a revelation and creation." But done day in and day out, like all repetitious work, it "becomes tiresome, empty, and monotonous." [24] Moreover, in her view, all tasks associated with raising children are tiresome, empty, and monotonous. She even refers to the tasks as "training," adding "[t]hat the child is the supreme aim of woman is a statement having precisely the value of an advertising slogan." [25]

A more important question for our purposes is how Beauvoir's account thus far offers insight regarding a possible distinction between sex and gender. In fact, she seems instead to conflate the two, suggesting that women are uniquely suited and biologically fated to a life of boring domesticity. Given their sex, their gender is one that emphatically precludes the projects that make men human beings. Yet, debilitating and monotonous as Beauvoir thinks women's biological life is, she rejects the idea that it suffices on its own to explain women's failure to pursue a more human existence. Rather, she argues that biological conditions are significant only in connection with specific economic, cultural, and social developments. Suppose, for example, that women are naturally weaker than men and have "less firmness and less steadiness."[26] These circumstances are important only in relation to certain aims. Indeed, if men are largely responsible for establishing economic, cultural, and social worlds, it is no wonder that these worlds play to their strengths and capacities rather than to women's. If a community thinks that its members must eat meat, then a man's strength and quickness in big-game hunting may be important. If, however, the community decides grains are more important, then that strength and quickness matters not at all. For Beauvoir, in consequence, mere biological conditions are important only because of the way human beings take them up. To the extent that women's biological sex plays any role in their subordination to men, it results not from intrinsic characteristics of that biology but rather from social and economic institutions as well as cultural practices that cater to a male rather than a female biology.[27]

In *The Second Sex*, sociological and psychological explanations for women's "immanence," or inability to transcend "life" for "existence," reinforce anthropological and historical ones. Take attitudes toward little boys' genitals. Beauvoir largely dismisses the Freudian conception of penis envy, according to which little girls are supposed to recognize early on that they lack a crucial appendage—namely, a penis—and are accordingly meant to envy little boys their possession of one. At the same time, Beauvoir thinks that boys do benefit from possessing penises, because adults make such a fuss about them. Even modest women, Beauvoir remarks, "give a nickname to the little boy's sex, speaking to him of it as of a small person who is at once himself and other than himself."[28] The penis becomes an incarnation of the boy, a projection of himself outward that allows him to "assume an attitude of subjectivity," an attitude of effective action. It is "a symbol of autonomy, of transcendence, of power."[29] In contrast, a little girl's elders do not typically fuss over her genitals, give them names, or direct the girl's attention to them. The result, Beauvoir says, is that the little girl does not "incarnate herself in any part of herself" as little boys do. Instead, she receives and plays with dolls. But dolls are importantly different from penises: They represent a girl's entire body, and they are objects. "The little girl coddles her doll and dresses her up as she dreams of being coddled and dressed up herself; inversely she thinks of herself as a marvelous doll."[30] Of course, boys can play with doll-analogues, and girls can use dolls in various different ways. Nevertheless, Beauvoir insists that

[t]he great advantage enjoyed by the boy is that his mode of existence
in relation to others leads him to assert his subjective freedom...He
undertakes, he invents, he dares. Certainly he tests himself as if he
were another; he challenges his own manhood...What is very important is that there is no fundamental opposition between his concern
for that objective figure which is his, and his will to self-realization in
concrete projects. It is by *doing* that he creates his existence, both in
one and the same action.[31]

In place of doing and creating, little girls wait. They are socialized into
a world of women in which they learn to let men take the lead and to occupy
themselves with sedentary activities. Sigmund Freud sees the Electra complex as a complement to the Oedipus complex. In resolving the latter, the
little boy gives up the loving attachment to his mother and learns to identify
with his father. Meanwhile, he holds his affection in reserve for the woman
he will eventually marry. Likewise, Freud assumes girls must resolve their
Electra complex—or in other words, their love for their fathers—so that ultimately, they can redirect it toward another man. Beauvoir, however, understands the Electra complex in different terms: For her, it marks the point at
which the little girl realizes that her father holds all of the power and that her
mother holds none. Furthermore,

[e]verything helps to confirm this hierarchy in the eyes of the little
girl. The historical and literary culture to which she belongs, the songs
and legends with which she is lulled to sleep, are one long exaltation
of man. It was men who built up Greece, the Roman Empire, France,
and all other nations, who have explored the world and invented the
tools for its exploitation, who have governed it, who have filled it with
sculptures, paintings, works of literature...thus it is that through the
eyes of men the little girl discovers the world and reads therein her
destiny.[32]

Ultimately, women find that they are the "Other." Because the world
is established by men for men, women occupy space in it only as inessential elements and only in relation to men. Beauvoir claims, "No group
ever sets itself up as the One without setting up the Other over against
itself...Jews are 'different' for the anti-Semite, Negroes are 'inferior' for
American racists, aborigines are 'natives' for colonists, proletarians are the
'lower class' for the privileged."[33] In some cases, the Other regards the One
as Other: the French are Other to the British, just as the British are Other
to the French. In these cases, there is what Beauvoir calls "reciprocity." In
other cases, such as those of Jews, blacks, aborigines, and proletarians, one
group dominates another and turns it into the "Other" for long and uncon-
scionable periods of time. Nevertheless, even in these cases, there is a time

before Otherness—before slavery, imperialism, or the like. Furthermore, Beauvoir insists, Jews, blacks, aborigines, and proletarians eventually band together and become Ones, rebelling against their oppression and becoming active subjects of their own futures.

What distinguishes women, Beauvoir argues, is that there is no historical period "before" Otherness and none after it; women never emerge. They have no history of independence and no economic separation from men. Instead, they rely on men for their livelihood and thus "lack concrete means for organizing themselves into a unit." Moreover, despite their shared biological sex, women occupy different social and economic positions and possess different races, nationalities, and the like:

> They live dispersed among the males, attached through residence, housework, economic condition, and social standing to certain men— fathers or husbands—more firmly than they are to other women. If they belong to the bourgeoisie, they feel solidarity with men of that class, not with proletarian women; if they are white, their allegiance is to white men, not to Negro women.[34]

Here, Beauvoir hints at the intersection of gender with race and class that will preoccupy later feminists and that we shall take up again in Chapter Four. In connection with establishing women's otherness, Beauvoir uses racial and class differences among women to argue that women construct no common basis for solidarity and therefore are at least partially complicit in their fate. While blacks, Jews, and the working class band together with other blacks, Jews, or proletarians to challenge and overcome their subordination, women do not. Instead, in the main, they ignore their commonality as women and disperse themselves among men, even binding themselves to those men through ties of love.[35] Moreover, Beauvoir maintains, to the extent that women do conceive of themselves primarily as women, they find the passivity it involves seductive. The songs and legends that "lull" women to sleep are pretty fairy tales. Indeed, Snow White and Sleeping Beauty sleep until their princes come to awaken them, while Cinderella endures until her prince bestows a glass slipper upon her foot. As Beauvoir summarizes, "Woman may fail to lay claim to the status of subject because she lacks definite resources, because she feels the necessary bond that ties her to man regardless of reciprocity, and because she is often very well pleased with her role as the *Other*."[36]

In *The Second Sex*, the implicit dichotomy between gender and sex thus consorts with a series of other dichotomies: between existence and life, subject and Other, transcendence and immanence, and freely chosen projects that move into the future versus ways of life that repeat substantially unchanged. Female children are socialized to become feminine women, who are the Other of men and who have been mired in immanence ever since those whom Beauvoir calls the "primitive hordes" first imposed a gendered division of labor based on differences in biological sex.

TREATING THE INTERSEXED

In saying that one is not born but rather becomes a woman, Beauvoir is interested in the processes by which biological females become what Rubin later calls "domesticated" women. John Money and Anke Ehrhardt also make a distinction between sex and gender. They do not do so implicitly, as Beauvoir does, but rather explicitly. For this reason, Ruth Hubbard credits them with popularizing the distinction.[37] More to the point, Money and Ehrhardt use the distinction not to explore and question sexism but rather to examine the development of what they call "gender identity," by which they mean the sense one has of being a man, a woman, or in some cases, ambivalent about who one is. Money and Ehrhardt are not concerned to provide a basis for women's equality or women's struggles. Rather, they are concerned with the intersexed: what should we do with infants who are born with genitalia that are either both male and female or neither clearly male nor clearly female? What should we do about their genitalia, and how should we raise the children, as girls or as boys?

Money and Ehrhardt define sex as "the reproductive capacity of the sex organs"[38] and claim "nature herself supplies" differences between male and female human beings.[39] They define gender identity as "the sameness, unity, and persistence of one's individuality as male, female, or ambivalent, in greater or less degree, especially as it is experienced in self-awareness and behavior."[40] For its part, gender role is "everything that a person says and does, to indicate to others or to the self the degree that one is either male, or female, or ambivalent."[41] Here, gender identity is the private experience of gender role, and gender role is the public expression of gender identity.[42] Gender is the combination of the two: gender identity and gender role. Moreover, Money and Ehrhardt claim that whereas sex involves "basic irreducible elements...which no culture can eradicate,"[43] gender (the combination of gender identity and gender role) is the result of socialization and, especially, the result of the influence of one's parents.

Money and Ehrhardt thus distinguish explicitly between biology and culture, sex and gender. Beauvoir and, after her, Rubin conceive of gender conventions as ways of dealing with and organizing sex. Indeed, Beauvoir suggests that existing social institutions and cultural conventions have the form they have in order to play to male biological strengths. In contrast, Money and Ehrhardt do not conceive of gender as a way of organizing the raw material of bodies. Instead, they see sex and gender as fundamentally distinct. Sex has to do with biology, and gender is a set of roles, functions, and ways of thinking about who one is that depend on interactions with other people, especially parents.

The upshot of this way of distinguishing sex and gender is a radical one. If one's sex depends on nature and one's gender on one's interactions with other people, then we have a clear strategy for treating intersexed conditions. Money and Ehrhardt claim that their research shows gender identity develops gradually. If one is not born but rather becomes a woman, one is also not born but rather becomes a girl, and one does so only gradually. At least up until about eighteen months of age, one's gender identity is malleable. Money and Ehrhardt also argue that for infants with ambiguous genitalia, this so-called gender identity gate of eighteen months opens up possibilities. It means that pediatricians and parents can decide whether to raise such infants as boys or as girls and that they can turn to surgeons to craft the appropriate genitalia. In addition, psychologists can be brought in to assist parents with bringing up the child in a way that reinforces the selected sex and encourages the appropriate gender identity and gender roles. Money and Ehrhardt think that the earlier corrective genital surgery is performed, the better, if only because it helps parents to raise their children in an unambiguously masculine or feminine way, without daily having to confront sexually ambiguous bodies. Nonetheless, as long as the correct procedures are put in place by eighteen months, "one may begin with the same clay and fashion a god or a goddess."[44]

In 1966, a tragic incident gave Money an opportunity to test this claim on a non-intersexed child.[45] When an eight-month old Canadian boy, Bruce Reimer, went to the hospital for a routine circumcision, an inexperienced practitioner shaved off most of his penis with an electrocautery machine. Bruce's parents, a young couple, were at a loss for what to do until they happened to see Money on a television show and decided to ask his advice. Relying on his work with intersexed infants, Money was clear in his recommendation: Bring up Bruce as a girl, remove the remaining parts of his penis, give him hormones, and at the appropriate time, create a fake vagina for him. The Reimers agreed, changing Bruce's name to Brenda, growing out her hair, and arranging for a bilateral orchidectomy to remove both testicles and the rest of the penis and for a series of consultations with psychologists. For Money, the case was especially intriguing, because it included a built-in experimental control against which to evaluate Brenda's progress as a girl: Bruce had an identical twin, Brian, with whom Brenda, despite being raised as a girl, would remain genetically identical. The situation thus presented an ideal test case for tracing the different effects of sex and gender, biology and upbringing. Indeed, if Brenda forged a successful gender identity as a girl, and if Brian did so as a boy, Money would have shown decisively that nurture outweighs nature. For this reason, Money arranged to meet with both children once a year throughout their childhood as a means of monitoring their psychosexual development and testing his views.

In the scientific journals where he published the results of these yearly meetings, Money claimed that the experiment was an unmitigated success. Despite her genetic identity with Brian, Brenda Reimer was a "normal" girl. She thought of herself as a girl, and she enjoyed typically feminine activities, such as "sewing, cleaning, dusting and doing dishes."[46] She also liked to maintain a neat appearance and played with typical girls' toys.[47] Thus, while Beauvoir distinguishes between the sex with which one is born and the gender that one becomes, Money insists the Reimer case shows that we can become whatever gender our parents and doctors want us to become, as long as they make their decision early enough in our lives. Although she would not endorse this kind of medical or parental intervention, Judith Butler suggests that this sort of radical disjunction between sex and gender is a logical consequence of Beauvoir's original distinction:

> If the distinction is consistently applied, it becomes unclear whether being a given sex has any necessary consequence for becoming a given gender...If being a woman is one cultural interpretation of being female, and if that interpretation is in no way necessitated by being female, then it appears that the female body is the arbitrary locus of the gender "woman," and there is no reason to preclude the possibility of that body becoming the locus of other constructions of gender. At its limit, then, the sex/gender distinction implies a radical heteronomy of natural bodies and constructed genders with the consequence that "being" female and "being" a woman are two very different sorts of being.[48]

CRITICIZING MONEY

Not everyone agrees with this "radical heteronomy," however. In fact, many argue that the empirical evidence simply refutes the claim that sex and gender are two very different features of individuals and that "'being' female and 'being' a woman are two very different sorts of being." Nor do they even agree with Beauvoir or with Money and Ehrhardt that socialization is responsible for turning biologically female children into women. Instead, they insist that when we look more carefully at the issue, we can see that feminism's much vaunted gender is caused by sex and amounts to no more than a reflection of it. For some of these critics, the ultimate outcome of Money's experiment with Bruce/Brenda proves the case.

As Brenda moved into adolescence, she began to resist Money's monitoring and staunchly refused to have a series of operations that were meant to create the fake vagina. Money, Brenda's parents, and a series of psychologists spent some years trying to coax her into the operation, but she never agreed. Finally, after an especially fierce battle, the Reimers gave up the fight and informed Brenda of her circumcision accident as well as her subsequent operations and gender reassignment. Brenda immediately stopped taking the hormones Money had prescribed, switched to testosterone, and began living as a boy, adopting the name David rather than returning to Bruce. Later, he had a double mastectomy as well as various operations to rebuild a penis, and he married a woman with two children of her own.

In fact, despite Money's published reports about the success of his experiment, outside observers had always suspected that not all was as rosy as he had claimed. Through interviews and their own observations, they found that Brenda did not actually play with dolls, despised the dresses her mother made for her, wrestled with Brian, and wanted to be a garbage man when she grew up. Relatives and teachers could later recall nothing feminine about her. A teacher remembered only "a rough-and-tumble rowdiness" and an "assertive, pressing dominance."[49] Others said Brenda was more interested in Brian's toys than her own and became a good shot with Brian's pellet rifle. As Brian himself noted, "She'd get a skipping rope for a gift, and the only thing we'd use that for was to tie people up, whip people with it…This sewing machine she got just sat."[50] Psychiatrists involved in the case reported that she had "a very masculine gait"[51] and, perhaps most disturbingly, preferred to urinate from a standing position.[52] Together with Brenda's ultimate transition to a masculine gender, these proclivities proved to many of Money's critics that despite his and the Reimers' attempts to mold a "goddess" out of the clay that was Bruce, Brenda remained a "god," gravitating toward masculine activities and explicitly taking up a masculine gender identity as David as soon as he could. Nature had won out, according to Money's critics, proving precisely the point that Money had wanted to refute.

Money's hypothesis was also the target of a larger study about the implications of sex for gender role and identity. In the 1970s, a group of researchers became interested in incidents of 5-alpha reductase deficiency that clustered in three rural villages of the Dominican Republic.[53] 5-Alpha reductase deficiency is a condition in which fetuses with XY chromosomes do not make as much dihydrotestosterone, a prenatal form of testosterone, as fetuses with XY chromosomes typically do. Fetuses affected by the deficiency fail to develop fully male organs in utero and are born with what can appear to be somewhat outsized clitorises. Although such infants may be raised initially as girls, large amounts of testosterone begin to course through their bodies at puberty, and they develop penises, deep voices, and hair that grows according to male patterns. The researchers in the Dominican Republic study focused on the gender consequences of these developments. Did those with the condition continue to identify and act as girls after their bodies changed, or did they adopt masculine gender identities and gender roles? The researchers assumed that if the individuals continued to live and identify as girls, this fact would confirm Money and Ehrhardt's view: Gender would indeed float free of sex and be a question only of upbringing. If, however, the individuals took up masculine identities and roles, then the researchers hypothesized that this fact would directly refute Money and Ehrhardt's view, showing that gender is biologically linked.

The researchers identified thirty-eight individuals with the condition, then focused on the nineteen who had initially been brought up as girls. Of these nineteen, the researchers said seventeen took up a masculine gender identity after puberty; sixteen of the seventeen also took up masculine gender roles, becoming farmers and woodsmen and admitting to sexual interest in women; and fifteen of the seventeen even had common law wives.[54] Based on these results, the researchers concluded that Money and Ehrhardt were dead wrong. Gender is not independent of sex; rather, gender follows directly from it.

A 2004 study reaffirmed these conclusions by examining fourteen genetic males reared as girls. The males were all born with cloacal exstrophy, a condition that can lead bladder, genital, and pelvic anomalies, including extremely small penises or even none at all: "phallic inadequacy or phallic absence" in the language of the study.[55] Like David Reimer, the infants in the study had all received orchidectomies, performed when they were between two and twelve weeks old. The study itself consisted of six questionnaires meant to assess psychosexual development, sexual identity, and gendered behavior. The duration of annual follow-up assessments ranged from two to eight years. At the end of the study, only four of the genetic males "declared unwavering female identity."[56] One was ambivalent, one refused to discuss sex or gender at all, and eight "declared unwavering male identity."[57] Moreover, four of this last group had done so spontaneously at the ages of seven, nine, nine, and twelve years, and even though the parents of two of these children had rejected their declarations. The other four had declared male identity upon hearing of their condition; these four did so at the ages of five, seven, seven, and eighteen. Like Money's critics in the David Reimer case and the Dominican Republic study, these authors suggest that when a child's biological sex differs from the gender identity and gender roles with which that child is raised, biological sex wins.

SUPPORTING MONEY

Does biological sex really win? Given the results of the studies described above, the "gender is an expression of sex" and "nature trumps nurture" camp would seem to have beaten their opponents in the Beauvoir and Money, "gender is separate from sex" and "nurture trumps nature" camp. However, the latter camp has weapons of its own.

Suppose we look at the David Reimer's case one more time. The evidence that notwithstanding his genital surgery and feminine upbringing, he failed to acquire a feminine gender identity or take up feminine roles rests on his allegedly masculine behavior, attitudes, and interests. After all, he liked to play with guns, hated dolls, and whipped people with jump ropes. Yet, must we assume that these attitudes and activities are necessarily a result of biology? Evidence that came to light after the Reimer case became public included the fact that Brenda's parents forced her to wear dresses even in freezing Winnipeg weather, when other little girls were wearing pants; that her father drank; and that her mother tried to commit suicide. Perhaps even worse, the visits that Brenda and Brian made to Money once a year for monitoring purposes turned out to be opportunities for Money to engage in a series of decidedly perverted actions, including the insistence that they remove their clothes to inspect each other's genitals and demonstrate the missionary position for making love.[58] Might "Brenda's" rough and obstreperous behavior be less evidence of biology than a symptom of the sort of stress she was under—of pressure from her parents to live up to their idea of what a little girl was, and pressure from Money to live out his own bizarre fantasies? And what about Brenda's preference for standing to urinate? Money claims that because of her genital surgery, Brenda's urine left her body at an awkward angle, and she had to be taught to press with her fingers in certain ways in order to urinate sitting down. It seems odd, then, to suppose that her urinating preferences have sex and/or gender implications. Surely, they might just as easily indicate problems with her bilateral orchidectomy.

What about the Dominican Republic study, which seemed to show that biological sex trumps the gender of rearing, even when the effects of biology kick in only during adolescence? The initial study claimed that nineteen of the children had been unambiguously raised as girls, but a later group of researchers who re-examined the data are not so sure. Cases of 5-alpha reductase deficiency were frequent enough in the villages under study to be a well-anticipated, familiar phenomenon. The inhabitants even had a name for it: *guevedoche*, or penis-at-twelve. Consequently, if an infant's genitalia seemed to differ at all from standard shapes or sizes, those parents may well have decided not to engage in full-scale gender socialization until they were sure whether the child was a *guevedoche* or not. In fact, when talking about their early childhoods, some of the subjects themselves recalled being uncomfortable about their genitalia, because they knew they did not look the same as other children's.[59] Many commentators also point to a striking difference in the lives of men and women in the villages under study. Men and boys had considerable amounts of free time, and truth be told, they often spent it in bars. In contrast, women and girls spent most of their time in daily chores and domestic duties. Conceivably, then, many or even most of the individuals who adopted male gender identities and roles did not do so because their biology superseded their upbringing. Rather, they may have done so because they could readily comprehend the freer and less dreary lives they would lead as men. In effect, they used the opportunity that their new penises afforded them to get out of the house.[60]

The 2004 study of cloacal exstrophy cases in which genetic males were raised as girls is also less definitive than Money's opponents might wish. In 2005, Heino F. L. Meyer-Bahlburg published the results of a study that looked at publications in English, German, and French from 1966 to 2004 involving gender assignment and cloacal exstrophy or related conditions in children, adolescents, and adults.[61] As of the most recent reports that Meyer-Bahlburg could find, sixty-nine percent of the children assigned to a feminine gender were living as girls, ninety-one percent of the adolescents assigned to a feminine gender were living as girls, and sixty-five percent of the adults so assigned were living as women.[62] Meyer-Bahlburg also ran the numbers excluding any individual that he thought might have been experiencing "gender dysphoria"—or in other words, a possible lack of comfort with the gender in which they were living. Using these numbers, he found that sixty-two percent of the children assigned to a feminine gender could be said to be living comfortably as girls, along with sixty-eight percent of the adolescents and forty-seven percent of the adults.[63] As those who may have been experiencing gender dysphoria grew older, there was "a modest trend of an increasing number...switching to male."[64] Nevertheless, Meyer-Bahlburg concludes, "Even by adulthood...at least about half maintained their female gender, including patients who were fully aware of their medical history."[65] Yet, if half maintained their female gender, then the jury is still out on whether sex trumps gender or not.

Meyer-Bahlburg also worries about the quality of the assessment methods that most of the reports he surveyed used, and he criticizes the 2004 study in particular for what he called "serious methodological flaws."[66] According to Meyer-Bahlburg, the 2004 study inferred masculine behavior from only "a few selected individual items" and based crucial data on gender dysphoria and gender change "on unsystematic follow-up communications with the parents" rather than with the affected individuals themselves.[67] The 2004 study also failed to employ independent methods of verifying its authors' evaluations of behaviors or even to use "masked co-rators"[68]—that is, evaluators who scored behaviors as masculine or feminine without knowing the purpose of the study. Indeed, Meyer-Bahlburg claims it is "remarkable"[69] that most of the cases he found of female-to-male gender change came from either the 2004 study or another study by the 2004 study's first author. Hence, he finds "future replication by independent investigators all the more important."[70]

Advocates of gender as separate from sex might stress additional peculiarities in the 2004 study. For instance, the study's authors found that only one of the XY children who were assigned the female sex played with dolls, and only "one ever played house."[71] Furthermore, "[p]arents noted substantial difficulty attempting to dress the subjects—but not their sisters—in clearly feminine attire after about four years of age."[72] Such play preferences and clothing difficulties are meant to suggest that the children possessed masculine gender identities or took up masculine gender roles. Yet, on what are these suggestions based? We have to presuppose that playing house, playing with dolls, and liking to wear dresses are feminine, but if so, are the conclusions of this study not circular? In other words, we know that children who do not like to play house show the gender effects of their male sex because they do not like to play house. The same circularity infects the assessment of Brenda Reimer's masculinity. For why, exactly, is it meant to be masculine to like to play with guns or whip people with ropes? And if the act of whipping people with ropes is meant to be masculine, should we not deplore masculinity in all individuals, not just poor Brenda Reimer?

INTERMEDIATE RECAP

We began this chapter with Gayle Rubin's explicit, and Simone de Beavoir's implicit, attempt to use a distinction between sex and gender to criticize the social, cultural, and economic position of women. We then looked at the controversies surrounding John Money and Anke Ehrhardt's insistence that sex and gender have absolutely nothing to do with one another. The meaning of gender undergoes a noticeable shift in this transition. Beauvoir and Rubin are concerned with the exclusion of females and women from civic and political institutions and practices. Gender in this connection pertains to the conventions that confine females and women to private, domestic functions and to such careers as social work and teaching, which might be said to expand the role of raising children to that of raising other people's children. In contrast, Money and Ehrhardt are concerned with the medical treatment of intersexed children and those who have suffered accidents to their penises. Gender in this connection pertains to one's sense of whether one is male or female (or not quite sure which) and to the roles that announce this identity to others. Yet, if the latter concerns and definition of gender stray from feminist concerns, they still have implications for them. For as we have seen, they raise persistent questions as to how sex and gender are, or are not, related. Furthermore, they raise questions about how we are to define the masculine and feminine genders at all. We pursue this latter question in Chapters Four and Five. In the remainder of this chapter, we continue examining how sex and gender go, or fail to go, together, and we do so first by turning to behavioral ecology, or what is more popularly known as sociobiology, and then by looking at hormones.

BEHAVIORAL ECOLOGY

In his 1994 book *The Moral Animal*, Robert Wright states that some feminists "now accept that men and women are deeply different." He continues:

> What exactly "deeply" means is something they're often vague about, and many would rather not utter the word genes in this context. Until they do, they will likely remain in a state of disorientation, aware that the early feminist doctrine of innate sexual symmetry was incorrect (and that it may have in some ways harmed women) yet afraid to honestly explore the alternative.[73]

Wright's alternative is that sex and gender go hand-in-hand, and that they do so for evolutionary reasons. We can begin, Wright says, with the observation that those of us who are alive today are here because we possess a genetic heritage that worked. Our oldest ancestors survived and reproduced ancestors who also survived and reproduced and, as the family tree continued, eventually produced us. Suppose, then, we ask what traits would have been useful for this survival and reproduction, and suppose that instead of thinking backward from hindsight, we think proactively: What do we have to do to maximize our chances of producing healthy children who can survive at least long enough to have children of their own, thereby allowing our genes to endure through successive generations? Wright claims that in species that reproduce sexually, males and females will have to answer this question in different ways depending on their reproductive roles. Because males and females have different biological roles in reproduction—that is, different sexes—they must devise different strategies to maximize the chances for the birth and survival of their offspring into maturity, and these strategies lead to different masculine and feminine traits—or in other words, to different genders.

Behavioral ecologists like Wright define females as those who produce large gametes or eggs for fertilization.[74] Human females do so, however, only relatively infrequently, and typically, they generate only one or perhaps two fertilized eggs. Moreover, the time between fertilization and birth is a long one, and to make matters worse, a female human being, once pregnant, cannot become more pregnant. Instead, she has to wait to give birth before she can start the process again. It follows, then, that female human beings have only limited opportunities to produce children. Moreover, in order to maximize their chances for children, they must make the most of the opportunities they have. Hence, they must be careful in their mating decisions, taking up only the most promising opportunities, where "promising" means those opportunities that bode well along two dimensions: First, those with whom females deign to mate must have the potential to produce healthy offspring and, second, these mates must also be both willing and able to provide sufficient resources to help nurture those offspring to maturity.

Males, for behavioral ecologists, are those who, in contrast to females, produce small gametes or sperm. In comparison to the rate at which human females can produce eggs and the effort it takes to do so, human males produce large amounts of sperm both easily and repeatedly. Nor does the circumstance that they may have already impregnated one female limit their ability to impregnate another—indeed, countless others. If males are to try to guarantee that they will produce healthy children who survive into adulthood, their strategy must therefore be quite different from that of females. Indeed, like the proverbial voters in Chicago whom the Daley machine urged to vote early and often, males should also mate early and often, trying to produce as many offspring as possible with the hope that one or more will live to adulthood and carry on their line. Thus, Wright says, we see the evolutionary function of two readily observable gender traits that follow directly from biology. Men, because of their biology, will be promiscuous and possess an interest in maximizing the quantity of mating opportunities irrespective of their quality. Women, because of their different biology, will be choosey and possess an interest in pursuing only the best mating opportunities, not the most. The same holds for mammals in general, Wright insists. To be sure, Wright concedes, female chimpanzees and especially female bonobos "seem particularly amenable to a wild sex life."[75] Yet, he insists, they do not do what males of the species do—namely, "search high and low, risking life and limb, to find sex, and to find as much of it, with as many different partners, as possible."[76] As Wright concludes, "Male license and (relative) female reserve are to some extent innate."[77]

Behavioral ecologists are adept at showing additional gender consequences of these strategies. For example, in keeping with an evolutionary history in which the males of the species follow bonobos in searching "high and low, risking life and limb, to find sex," one would expect men to be better than women with numbers, maps, and spatial analysis. And, indeed, some research seems to confirm this expectation. Men have been observed to perform better on mental rotation tests, in which subjects are asked to rotate figures drawn on paper through three dimensions;[78] on spatial tests, in which they are asked to throw and intercept balls;[79] and in virtual maze tests, in which they are asked to learn a novel route through a three-dimensional map.[80] In all cases, males performed the tasks more quickly and more accurately than females, even when controlling for such factors as more experience and, in the last case, more time spent playing computer games. In fact, a thirty-year study published in the late 1990s found that in tests of math and science ability, boys outnumbered girls in the top ten percent by three to one and, furthermore, that "in the top 1 percent, there were seven boys for every one girl."[81]

Behavioral ecologists often attribute these results to differences in the way the brain structures of men and women have evolved. The human male cerebrum is nine percent bigger than the female cerebrum, while the ratio of corpus callosum to total cerebrum volume is smaller in males.[82] The male amygdala also grows for an extended period during childhood and is larger than that in the female. Finally, the male cerebral cortex has more neurons than the female cerebral cortex, and they tend to be more tightly packed. This fact suggests that more connections between neurons occur within one hemisphere in men with "decreased interhemispheric connectivity," while women are more "bilateral."[83] Behavioral ecologists trace the explanation for both sets of differences to the brain organizations that would have won out in the evolutionary environment. Women, not racing around the evolutionary environment trying to impregnate people, need not have processed spatial relations as efficiently as men. As a result, they use both sides of the brain to control spatial skills. Hence, each side of their brains must deal with interferences from the activities that the other side may be trying to control. Male brains, in contrast, control spatial abilities more locally, leaving less chance for other activities to interfere.[84]

QUESTIONING BEHAVIORAL ECOLOGY

Just as no good deed goes unpunished, no scientific study goes unquestioned. Take studies of differences in male and female brains and cognition. The late

1990s study showed persistent differences in the mathematical and spatial abilities of boys and girls, but a study published in 2001 reconsidered these results.[85] Using two longitudinal surveys of American children, researchers examined the children's mathematical paths from first through twelfth grade. Few differences were found between boys and girls up to about eleven years of age, but at age eleven, girls posted higher average scores. When researchers examined only the scores of the children scoring most highly on the mathematical tests, they found that between the ages of four and seven, girls in this group scored higher than boys in this group; between the ages of eight to eleven, the boys scored higher than the girls; and between the ages of eleven and thirteen, there were no statistically significant differences in the scores of the children in the group. With regard to the reasoning skills in this oldest high-scoring group, girls had a slight advantage. In older, college-age individuals, the study found a small and statistically insignificant difference, with male students scoring higher in both math and reasoning. Only with regard to spatial skills in the area of geometry did the study find statistically significant differences, but even these decreased once the girls were taught spatial strategies.

Suppose, however, the studies showed that men did have better math and spatial abilities than women. Would that discovery provide a definitive answer to the question of sex versus gender? In one test for spatial abilities, subjects sit on chairs in darkened rooms with rods balanced within large frames in front of them. Each subject's task is to keep the rod perpendicular to the floor as a researcher tilts either the frame or the chair. In seven of twelve studies that researchers examined, men performed better on this task than women.[86] We could point out that in five studies, they did not, but we should also recall that traditionally, boys, but not girls, receive models to build and blocks to play with when they are growing up. Might not another explanation be that for social and cultural reasons, women are distracted and ill at ease in dark rooms, perhaps especially when male investigators surround them?[87]

While conventional wisdom says that boys are better in math and with maps, it also says that girls are better with verbal tasks. The same thirty-year study that found boys to be better in math found girls to be better in reading comprehension and writing, with twice as many girls as boys found among the top scorers and twice as many boys as girls among the bottom.[88] But, if women's comparative weakness in math and spatial abilities all but disappears in recent research, and if we attribute the remaining disparities to cultural factors, what explains boys' comparative weaknesses in reading and writing? Both are required across the elementary and high school curricula, and for this reason alone, a cultural explanation for the gender disparity would seem to be less than plausible. Michael Kimmel thinks it is the correct explanation anyway. Boys' comparative weakness in reading and writing tests, he says, is part of the "ideology of traditional masculinity."[89] Unless they are poets or novelists, men, as a gender, are not meant to be good with words. "What makes a man a man," Kimmel writes, "is that he is reliable in a crisis and what makes a man reliable in a crisis is that he resembles an inanimate object."[90]

HORMONE STUDIES

In the popular imagination, the part of biological sex that is often thought to exert the most influence on gender is hormonal. Indeed, when they were first discovered in the 1920s, the so-called "sex hormones" were supposed to be all-purpose explanations: Men were men because their bodies possessed testosterone; women were women because their bodies possessed estrogen. It even looked like homosexuality could be explained as an atypical invasion of estrogen into a man's body, whereas agitation for female suffrage could be explained as an atypical invasion of testosterone into a woman's.[91] The hormones themselves were named after the respective sex to which they attached: androgens from the Greek word for men (*andros*) and estrogens from the English word, estrus, referring to the period immediately preceding ovulation. (Forget for the moment that the hormones associated with the male sex get to derive their name from man while estrus comes from the Latin, *oestrus*, meaning frenzy or gadfly, and from the Greek, *oistros*, meaning gadfly, sting, or mad impulse.[92]) Research today largely rejects the role of hormones on sexuality or female suffrage, but some studies, and certainly the popular imagination, continue to appeal to hormones as a cause for differences in gender. In particular, testosterone is said to lead to what are meant to be the masculine traits of dominance, persistence, energy, libido, and focused attention. One analysis even attributes Celestine's failed papacy in 1294, a papacy that lasted less than five months, to his low baseline level of testosterone.[93]

Behavioral ecologists offer us a different explanation for testosterone's importance: men would have benefited from sudden bursts of it in pursuing their "live fast and die young" lifestyle, clambering over other males and beating them down to impregnate the available females. Andrew Sullivan is especially rhapsodic about testosterone, linking it to "confidence, competitiveness, tenacity, strength and sexual drive."[94] Noting that he must give himself regular injections of a synthetic version of it for medical reasons ("a biweekly encounter with a syringe full of manhood," as he puts it[95]), Sullivan credits testosterone with an increase in appetite, far less need for sleep, and a complete absence of the depression he says used to plague him. He also feels "better able to recover from life's curve balls, more persistent, more alive." In Sullivan's view, what he calls the "Big T" explains the "deeply male" substitution of risk and intense experience for security and longevity, and it "affects every aspect of our society from high divorce rates and adolescent violence to the exploding cults of bodybuilding and professional wrestling."[96]

Anne Moir and David Jessel suggest the opposite effects of estrogen:

> Colin is a quiet boy. He is studious, shy, and tries to avoid games...He has no interest in contact sports. If there's a free-for-all in the playground, Colin simply walks away from it. His mother, who tells him he "should stand up for himself," says that in sixteen years he has only once been involved in a fight. Colin's mother, it transpires, took doses of synthetic female hormone during pregnancy.[97]

Not to be outdone, researchers also examine effects on girls whose mothers took a course of synthetic progestins with androgen-like characteristics during pregnancy. Here, Erika serves as an example:

> She likes rough-and-tumble games, chase games, and activities involving climbing—and trespassing. She dresses in boys' clothes, and prefers their company. She has only once taken her doll out of the cupboard, and that was to put it into the bath "to see if it would float." Her schoolteachers complain of her rowdiness. She frequently starts fights, and is known to have a frequent, and violent temper. She is more self-confident, self-reliant, domineering and ambitious.[98]

The link between testosterone, aggression, and "manhood" is also supposed to show up in comparisons strictly between men, between those with more machismo and those with less. Thus, a 1998 study of male lawyers found what the *New York Times* calls "juris cojones."[99] It turns out that male trial lawyers have higher testosterone levels than other lawyers, even male ones. In fact, according to James Dabbs, the lead author of the study, trial lawyers are so aggressive, they sometimes have to "tone down" their personalities or risk alienating the jury. "There's a certain animal quality to their behavior," he continues, "They're less concerned with pleasing other people."[100] Another study in 1992 measured serum levels of testosterone in former enlisted men who were representative of the United States population as whole in terms of race, education, income, and occupation.[101] What it found was that those with the higher testosterone levels were either unemployed or blue-collar workers, while those with lower testosterone levels were white-collar workers. Moreover, it linked high testosterone to "low verbal intelligence, antisocial behavior and insufficient education, all leading to low occupation status."[102] Of course, the link could go in either of two directions: either high testosterone levels might cause "low-status" jobs or low-status jobs might increase levels of testosterone. Or perhaps blue-collar workers have more physical confrontations with managers and co-workers, and perhaps these confrontations raise testosterone levels. Still, the study concluded that even if physical confrontations do raise testosterone levels in male blue-collar workers, the effect is not significant enough to explain the extent of the hormone differences between them and male white-collar workers. Testosterone, it seems, is "deeply male"—indeed, sometimes too deeply male. For Sullivan, in fact, testosterone "helps explain, perhaps better than any other single fact, why inequalities between men and women remain so frustratingly resilient in public and private life."[103]

What do critics of the "sex leads to gender" camp have to say, or what could they say, about hormone studies? Erika is meant to be masculine in wanting to see if her doll will float, in possessing a bad temper, and in being self-confident, self-reliant, domineering, and ambitious.[104] Yet, surely we need not think such characteristics are only, or even primarily, masculine. Indeed, rather than demonstrating Erika's masculinity, does the connection of all these characteristics to one another already presuppose it? Otherwise, why suppose the characteristics have anything to do with one another? Certainly, nothing about the trait of self-confidence would link it inherently to an experimental attitude about floating or to a bad temper. Nor is it clear why female hormones should explain Colin's penchant for non-violence. Should we question Mahatma Gandhi's masculinity or the levels of testosterone in male members of the Society of Friends? Indeed, we might ask whether testosterone is really all it is cracked it up to be. Take, for example, its effects in monkeys. Better yet, compare the neurobiologist Robert Sapolsky description of a monkey hierarchy to Sullivan's paean to "the Big T."[105] Sapolsky's description is worth quoting at length:

> Round up some male monkeys. Put them in a group together...Give them enough time to form a dominance hierarchy, the sort of linear ranking in which number 3, for example, can pass his day throwing around his weight with numbers 4 and 5, ripping off their monkey chow, forcing them to relinquish the best spots to sit in, but numbers 1 and 2 still expect and receive from him the most obsequious brown-nosing...Take that third-ranking monkey and give him some testosterone...inject a ton of it...give him enough testosterone to grow antlers and a beard on every neuron in his brain. And, no surprise, when you check the behavioral data, he will probably be participating in more aggressive interactions than before.
>
> So...testosterone causes aggression, right? Wrong. Check out number 3 more closely. Is he raining terror on everyone in the group,

frothing with indiscriminate violence? Not at all. He's still judiciously kowtowing to numbers 1 and 2 but has become a total bastard to numbers 4 and 5. Testosterone isn't causing aggression, it's exaggerating the aggression that is already there.[106]

We should stress two points in particular here. First, the levels of testosterone that the individual monkeys possess at the beginning of the experiment do not predict which monkey will be dominant or submissive in the hierarchy they establish. Second, flooding them with artificial testosterone does not change the focus of their aggressive behavior or make them assertive against those to whom they were previously submissive. Rather, individual monkeys simply treat in a worse way those they already treated badly.

Other studies show that testosterone rises and falls with emotions. If two tennis players have equal levels of testosterone before they play a match against one another, testosterone levels rise in the one who eventually wins and fall in the one who eventually loses.[107] When the American hostages were released from captivity in Iran in 1981 after 444 days of captivity, immediate physiological and psychological testing found measures of cortisol, catecholamine, and testosterone levels in the men to be extremely elevated. These reflected not aggression, however, but "three strong affects: distress, anxiety and elation."[108] We might also point out that the authors of the study associating higher levels of testosterone with men in lower-status jobs was stumped when it came to farmers. As it turns out, farmers have the lowest levels of testosterone of all, even lower than white-collar men. This "finding," the researchers admit, "presents a puzzle,"[109] since farming would seem to require toughness and white-collar jobs would seem to have a higher social status. But by way of an answer, the researchers only, and completely enigmatically, quote Willa Cather on the weather: "Men's affairs went on underneath it, as the streams creep under the ice."[110]

Despite it status in popular culture, testosterone is therefore a bit of a disappointment in the attempt explain gendered behaviors by way of biological sex. It is only fair, however, to point out that estrogen is equally disappointing. In 1934, Bernard Zondek discovered estrogen in the testicles of a virile stallion and, much to his own dismay, thereby destabilized the received understanding of hormones as responsible for masculine dominance and feminine submission. Zondek himself remained confused. "To this day," he said in an interview, "I do not understand how it is that the high concentration of estrogen in stallion testes and blood does not exert an emasculating effect." (The interviewer had a quick response: "It is fortunate for the stallion that he has no chance of knowing your trouble."[111])

CONCLUSION

Given persistent questions about and differences between scientific studies, what should we conclude about the relation between sex and gender? In recent decades, the unidirectional debate over whether or not sex characteristics cause gender traits has given way to a more reciprocal conception of the causal process. Carol Worthman notes that synthetic organic chemicals affect gonadal steroids and that diet affects hormones.[112] Anne Fausto-Sterling makes a similar point using bones: According to a recent study, maintaining at least an average weight is the best predictor of good bone mass density.[113] Yet, in another study of adolescents in the United States, 27 percent of girls who think they weigh the correct amount are nonetheless trying to lose weight, while only 10 percent of the boys who think they weigh the correct amount are trying.[114] We can assume that cultural conceptions of beauty are at work here. Yet, insofar as they affect our bones, they affect our relative weakness and strength, perhaps as much as hormones do. Indeed, it seems uncontroversial that cultural practices affect bodies. Just consider how much vitamin D women can absorb if they are outdoors on a sunny day but clothed in full burkas. On the other hand, Fausto-Sterling also argues that girls and boys may differ in basal metabolism rates that affect food intake. It looks, then, as if many factors, some cultural and some biological, contribute to bone density and to physical bodies in general. As Fausto-Sterling puts the point, "We are always 100 percent nature and 100 percent nurture."[115]

Numerous questions remain about the relation between sex and gender. Before considering them, however, perhaps we should ask how many of each there are.

CHAPTER TWO

Different Sexes; Different Genders

An old rhyme runs as follows:

Though they of different sexes be
On the whole they are the same as we
For those that have the strictest searchers been,
Find women are but men turned outside in.[1]

If we replace the word sexes with the word genders to reflect the distinction between the two that we have been discussing, then this doggerel describes a view of human biology that Thomas Laqueur claims held sway in Europe for almost two millennia—indeed, until the middle of the eighteenth century. To be sure, the rhyme also confirms Beauvoir's claim that men are the subjects of action and the authors of knowledge, while women are the Other: It is hard to overlook the dichotomy between "we," the group to whom the writer assumes his readers belong, and "they," the women who remain the Other. Nevertheless, the crux of the rhyme holds that men and women possess the same body. There is only one sex, even if there are two genders.

In this chapter, we look as a series of possibilities for conceiving of the numerical relations between sex and gender. We begin with one sex and two genders and subsequently turn to two sexes and three genders as well as to three sexes and two genders. Given these options, might we not legitimately stress the influence culture has on conceptions of both gender and sex? We begin in Europe.

THE ONE-SEX MODEL

According to Laqueur, the corporeal differences between men and women that a modern Western worldview sees as marking the existence of two distinct sexes are, in the premodern and early modern Western view, merely geographic: The same organs that are on the outside of male bodies are on the inside of female bodies. The vagina is an interior, inside-out penis that serves as the sheath into which the penis fits; the labia make for an interior foreskin; the uterus is an interior scrotum; and the ovaries are interior testicles. As Laqueur points out, Galen, the second-century Greek physician whose authority lasted until the late eighteenth century, even employed the same word for testes and ovaries: *orchesis*.[2]

Bodily fluids also failed to differentiate men and women in premodern and early modern Europe, Laqueur says. Instead, physicians and medical experts thought these fluids could convert into one another and therefore that what might look like distinct fluids in men and women were simply different forms of a single, endlessly protean substance. Sperm, for instance, was a residual fluid: "[F]irst refined out of the blood[,] it passed to the brain; from the brain it made its way back through the spinal marrow, the kidneys, the testicles, and into the penis."[3] Menstrual blood, for its part, was fluid converted from excess nutrition. Indeed, the reason that pregnant women did not menstruate was that they had no excess nutrition; their fetuses used up any leftovers these women might otherwise have had. Likewise, the reason nursing women did not menstruate was that their extra nutrition converted into milk for feeding the baby.

As these examples imply, fluids were thought to participate in what Laqueur calls "a free-trade economy."[4] Different secretions served to balance one another and to keep the overall level of fluids in the body at an appropriate level. Women menstruated less in the summer than in the winter, because in the summer, they perspired more and therefore had less bodily fluid available to transmute into blood.[5] Even sexual desire was a function of balancing fluids. A text from the late Middle Ages explained that the excess nutrition women accumulated in eating could lead to refinements from the blood that heated woman's vulva "and cause her greatly to desire coition."[6]

If men and women possessed identical fluids and organs, what explained the different positions their organs occupied in their bodies? Galen attributed this difference to temperature and humidity: Whereas men's bodies were hot and dry, women's bodies were cold and moist, and because they were, women's bodies lacked sufficient heat to force the organs to their proper place on the outside. In the end, for Galen (here following Aristotle), women were simply imperfect, outside-in men. The human body was a male body. If it lacked adequate warmth, it would become only half-baked, and things that ought to expand to the outside would remain internal. Moist and damp conditions also explained why, unless they were pregnant or nursing, women could not usefully employ all the nutrition they absorbed. Again, they lacked sufficient heat to burn it and, hence, had to excrete excesses in the form of blood.

Yet, despite their differences in temperature and humidity, men and women shared a body and consequently, Laqueur says, distinctions between them were considered perilous. In Shakespeare's *Romeo and Juliet*, for instance, when Romeo regrets his refusal to fight Tybalt, he rues the way in which Juliet's beauty has "soft'ned valour's steel." For Laqueur, this remark is more than a metaphor. Rather, falling in love with Juliet succeeds in making Romeo effeminate. Laqueur writes, "Bodies actually seem to slip from their sexual anchorage in the face of heterosexual sociability; being with women too much or being too devoted to them seems to lead to the blurring of what we would call sex."[7]

Women, too, risked changing sexes, especially if they engaged in male activities and became too hot as a consequence. Michel de Montaigne relates the case of Marie Garnier, a young woman who jumped across a ditch while chasing pigs and suddenly sprouted a penis.[8] Citing a sixteenth-century surgeon, Ambroise Paré, Laqueur writes, "Puberty, jumping, active sex or something else whereby 'warmth is rendered more robust' might be just enough to break the interior-exterior barrier and produce on a 'woman' the marks of a 'man.'"[9] In fact, women who possessed more bodily heat than normal were thought capable of producing semen.

How does conception occur according to the one-sex model? Different embryologists offered different theories, but according to Laqueur, they all agreed on the general outlines. If men and women shared a body, that body could perform in only one way. Whatever the male did, the female had to do as well, only on the inside instead of the outside:

> Both sexes experienced a violent pleasure during intercourse that was intimately connected with successful generation; both generally emitted something; pleasure was due both to the qualities of the substance emitted and to its rapid propulsion by "air"; the womb performed double duty in both emitting something and then drawing up and retaining a mixture of the two emissions.[10]

As much as the one-sex model may recall G. A. Strong's well-known spoof of Henry Wadsworth Longfellow's "Song of Hiawatha,"[11] Laqueur tells us that it would be a mistake to attribute the model merely to rudimentary and deficient medical and scientific knowledge. Scientists did make discoveries during the period in which the one-sex model ruled. Moreover, they made discoveries that could have undermined it. The Renaissance discovered the clitoris, for example, so at the very least, the one-sex model had to deal with two analogues to penises in women: the vagina and the clitoris.[12] Why, we might expect physicians to have asked, should women have two penises, an inside and an outside, if women were men "turned outside in" and men had only one? For that matter, if the womb had to perform "double duty in both emitting something and then drawing up and retaining a mixture of the two emissions" did that "fact" itself not signal a difference between male and female bodies? Did it not suggest the existence of two sexes? And what about the idea that conception required both male and female to emit a substance and, hence, required orgasms on both their parts? Was the observation that some women got pregnant without orgasms not sufficient to disprove this idea and, with it, the one-sex model?

According to Laqueur, we might just as easily move in the opposite direction and ask why the "facts" that later scientists discovered could not themselves have been interpreted within the terms of a one-sex model. After all, he explains, developments in the anatomical sciences during the nineteenth century "pointed to the common origins of both sexes in a morphologically androgynous embryo."[13] More to the point, perhaps, counterexamples to the one-sex model could always be re-explained. Take the idea that conception required the female to emit a substance and thus required female orgasm. How could physicians explain the phenomenon of women becoming pregnant without experiencing orgasms? Easy enough. The women who claimed to have conceived without having orgasms could simply be lying, insisting for reasons of modesty that although they may have had sexual intercourse, they certainly had not enjoyed it. Or take the case of the woman in a coma who suddenly turned up pregnant. Perhaps she was not as comatose as she at first appeared—or at least not comatose enough to avoid orgiastic reactions.[14] In both cases, the apparent fact— conception without orgasm—could be explained away simply by questioning other facts and thereby keeping the one-sex model intact.

So a better question to ask is why Westerners eventually modified their theories. Why did they move to a two-sex model in the late eighteenth century? Laqueur claims that for premodern and early modern Westerners, the body occupied a different conceptual space from the one it occupies for modern Westerners. The body was not a foundational bedrock on which various attributes could be attached. Instead, it was part of a cosmic order in which microcosm reflected macrocosm. One could offer dietary advice by mapping the signs of the zodiac onto the organs of the body; find correlates for the heavenly bodies in garden herbs;[15] and expect religious heretics to give birth to monsters.[16] One could also see the body as the reflection of a natural order, a developmental hierarchy with God at the top and a single line of development ascending from the bottom toward Him. Male and female bodies had to be the same body and, because both had to be part of the same ascending development, they had to represent it in more perfect forms (men's) and less perfect forms (women's). The feasibility of the one-sex model, then, lay in an entire web of belief. One could not modify the one-sex part of this web without causing havoc and necessitating changes in the rest of it.

The same metaphysical commitments applied to beliefs about conception. Here, Laqueur suggests, even though the one-sex model was able to solve the problem of conception without orgasm by simply denying the absence of orgasm, it did acknowledge another problem. For if both men and women possessed the same fluids as the one-sex model insisted, why did women need men at all to procreate? Why could they not simply conceive children on their own? After all, the visible signs of conception took place in their bodies. Fortunately, the belief in an ascending hierarchy provided the answer: Normal conception was the result of the male having something like an idea in a female's body, and because females were imperfect, they could have only weak or misbegotten ideas on their own. Isidore of Seville, a sixth-century encyclopedist, thus claimed that although conception without a father was possible, it could produce only brutes. Laqueur calls this claim less a claim about bodies than a claim about the power, legitimacy, and prerogatives of masculinity and fatherhood. As he writes, "In a public world that was overwhelmingly male, the one-sex model displayed what was already massively evident in culture more generally; man is the measure of all things, and women does not exist as an ontologically distinct category."[17]

When Western Europe finally did move toward a two-sex model, it did so in part, according to Laqueur, because science and religion parted ways, with the natural and biological worlds becoming increasingly denuded of any extrafactual significance. The body was simply a body, no longer an illustration of the cosmos, and the reproduction of the species no longer had to link up to a great chain of being.[18] Laqueur thinks that the reasons for this change were also partly political, connected to eighteenth-century worries about the changing status of women. To be sure, some feminists seized upon the new idea that there were actually two sexes to argue for women's rights to their own independent social and political voice. Women's views could be easily dismissed from the perspective of the one-sex model; after all, if men were essentially perfected versions of women, then men's social and political voices would surely be more perfect versions of women's own. In contrast, if there were actually two sexes, could feminists not use the difference between them to argue for the necessity of women representing and voicing their own views?

Despite the apparent logic here, the move to a two-sex model ultimately served the other side.[19] Because women were different from men, theorists and politicians argued that they needed to occupy a different domain from men. And because men belonged in the public and political world, women would have to belong to the private and domestic one. Moreover, as members of the private, domestic sphere, they were clearly mentally and physically unsuited to civic and public responsibilities. Rousseau encapsulates this view in *Emile* when he declares that men's and women's minds should be no more alike than their bodies and mandates that each receive a different form of education, one as the leader and the other as the led.[20]

Unsurprisingly, not everyone agrees with Laqueur's history. Some think he overemphasizes the hegemony of a one-sex model before the eighteenth century.[21] Lynda Coon, for example, maintains that medieval writers employed any means they could find to devalue women. Sometimes they availed themselves of a one-sex model that allowed them to call women inverted and defective, and sometimes they used a two-sex model that allowed them to privilege male bodies.[22] Conversely, other scholars think that Laqueur downplays the extent to which the one-sex model persisted into the nineteenth century. Alice Domurat Dreger, for example, cites the nineteenth-century idea that proto-labia formed in male and female fetuses but continued to develop in male fetuses and eventually joined together to form a scrotum. An underdeveloped male would therefore look female, and an overdeveloped female would look male.[23]

We might also question just how far we have traveled from a one-sex model and to what extent men remain the measure of all things human. What Laqueur himself stresses is the extent to which conceptions of sex go beyond empirical facts. The facts of the body are always interpretable ones. We never have an unconditioned access to the body that is not mediated by some prior, more global conceptions. In other words, we always see it *as* something—as an illustration of the cosmos, an imperfect man, or a separate but inferior sex. Laqueur quotes the so-called Quine-Duhem thesis: Knowledge "is so underdetermined by...experience that there is much latitude as to what statements to reevaluate in the light of any contrast experience."[24] To this extent, the move from a one-sex to a two-sex model has less to do with scientific progress than one might wish.

In subsequent chapters, we shall see how far some feminist theorists take these claims about knowledge and the body. Rather than providing increased insight regarding an unchanging, material bedrock, different scientific discourses simply construct what the body is. Laqueur, himself, pulls back a bit, claiming that in spite of the Quine-Duhem thesis, we ought not ignore either what he sees as the reality of the body or the increased ability of scientists to explain it. We clearly know more about our bodies than premoderns or early moderns knew about theirs, Laqueur says. "Women are much better able to predict the cyclical likelihood of pregnancy than their ancestors...Menstruation turns out to be a different physiological process than hemorrhoidal bleeding…and the testes *are* histologically different from the ovaries."[25] What his findings illustrate, Laqueur maintains, is simply the "space" between "the real transcultural body" and its "representations."[26] In other words, for Laqueur, there are real facts about our material bodies even though different cultures and traditions might represent these facts in different, and even rather odd, ways. In Chapter Three, we will return to ways in which feminists and women's studies scholars have examined such claims. In the rest of this chapter, however, we continue to explore various "representations" in models assuming three sexes with two genders, models assuming two sexes with three genders, and models assuming two sexes with two genders.

THREE-SEX MODELS

Premodern and Renaissance scientists were aware of the existence of hermaphrodites, or those now more commonly called intersexed.[27] Where did these authorities think the intersexed fell on the one-sex schema? It must have been fairly easy to describe the causes of hermaphrodism—namely, versions of the body that were warmer than female versions but colder than male versions. But concerns about hermaphrodism were not simply, or even primarily, medical. Instead, the real worry was where hermaphrodites fell on the scale of being and, hence, what their social and political status ought to be. If one were intersexed, ought one have the rights and entitlements of a man or the disenfranchised status of a woman? Or maybe one ought to have a status somehow in between the two.

Take the 1601 French case of Marie or Marin le Marcis, who possessed what was either a large clitoris or a small penis. Marie/Marin lived her life as a woman until she was twenty-one, at which point she decided to marry the woman she lived with and began wearing men's clothes. Arrested on two charges, sodomy and cross-dressing, she was condemned initially to burn at the stake and subsequently to a no-less-horrific sentence of death by strangling.[28] At some point, however, someone decided to ask medical authorities to determine what she/he actually was: male or female—or as Laqueur writes, whether the "candidate for an external penis entitled her to the prerogatives of penis possession."[29] The stakes were high, not only because of the death sentence but also because if the questionable appendage were really a penis, then Marie/Marin deserved "a promotion on the scale of being"[30] and ought to be granted the rights and entitlements of a man. Luckily for Marie/Marin, the appendage did pass muster as a penis, and she/he did qualify for a status promotion. Nevertheless, the authorities also, and somewhat mysteriously, ruled that she/he could qualify only gradually. They ordered Marie/Marin to live as a woman and wear women's clothes until the age of twenty-five and only then to take up life as a man.

An earlier case in 1459 did not have such a relatively happy ending. In this case, an intersexed individual lived most of her life as a woman but made the mistake of impregnating her employer's daughter, and for that, she was burned at the stake.[31] Evidently, her crime was not so much that she had tried for most of her life to pass as a woman without informing her employer or the medical authorities of her intersexed condition. Instead, her real crime was that having lived as a woman, she then presumed to have sex as a man.

In general, the problem that intersexed conditions posed for the one-sex model was not which sex to assign intersexed individuals. After all, there was only one sex to assign. Rather, the problem was which social rank intersexed people could and should assume. But if this was the problem that preoccupied the West, many anthropologists argue that other cultures found a different solution, assigning intersexed individuals their own third sex. Recall the Dominican Republic cases of 5-alpha reductase deficiency that we looked at in Chapter One. In studying these cases, researchers focused on whether or not the affected individuals changed their gender when they developed male sex characteristics. The initial study claimed that they did and, consequently, that biological sex is the determining factor in fixing gender identity. A subsequent study found the evidence for the causal role of biological sex less clear. Fewer of the affected individuals changed their gender than the original authors had claimed, and those who did may have done so for cultural reasons involving the circumstances of women in the affected villages. In his own remarks on the case, the anthropologist Gilbert Herdt takes a third tack. We ought not, or at least we ought not precipitously, he says, use the Dominican Republic case to argue for the causal role of either nurture or nature on gender identity. Rather, he finds it telling that the villagers had a word for those with the 5-alpha reductase deficiency, *guevedoche* or penis-at-twelve.[32] What this name indicates, Herdt thinks, is that those who changed their gender identities did not change from being young women to being young men. Instead, they changed from being *guevedoche* who were living as young girls to *guevedoche* who were living as men. In other words, the villages may have possessed a sex/gender system comprising three sexes—male, female, and *guevedoche*—and two genders—man and woman.

Herdt says he can offer only speculations on the Dominican Republic case, but he is more certain about a third sex among the Sambia in Papua New Guinea. Like the *guevedoche*, those whom the Sambia call *kwolu-aatmwol*, or "changing into a male thing," are born with 5-alpha reductase deficiency. However, Sambian society is quite different from Dominican society. Normally, boys are separated from their mothers sometime between the ages of seven and ten and go to live exclusively in the men's house. Here, they are prohibited from all contact with women and undergo a series of six initiations into male society that span a period of about fifteen years. The initiations are necessary because, according to Sambian belief, the possession of male genitalia does not yet constitute biological maleness. Rather, biological maleness requires the capacity to produce children, and this capacity is acquired only through repeated inseminations of younger boys by older ones. The first two initiations in the Sambian series are designed to accomplish this task. During the third initiation, the previous fellators are deemed sufficiently male to inseminate younger boys who are still in the first two stages of initiation. In the fourth initiation, the initiate is considered mature enough to receive a wife. The fifth initiation occurs when that wife begins to menstruate and the sixth when the couple has their first child.[33]

What marks the *kwolu-aatmwol* off from boys is that the *kwolu-aatmwol* never undergo the whole series of initiations. Those *kwolu-aatmwol* reared initially as girls because their genitalia looked female at birth miss out on the series entirely and remain in their mother's home during the crucial initiation years. Those *kwolu-aatmwol* reared initially as boys participate in the first two stages of initiation but are prevented from participating in the remaining three and, consequently, never become fully male. Herdt says he did discover one *kwolu-aatmwol* who apparently possessed political connections that allowed him to gain entry to the third stage of initiation. Yet, he was required to spend a longer-than-normal period in the first and second stages. Nor did he receive the ritual nosebleed that was part of the initiation series and considered necessary in order to release female fluids from a boy's body. Accordingly, he remained *kwolu-aatmwol* and never achieved full rank as a man.

Herdt does not contend that third sexes such as *guevedoche* and *kwolu-aatmwol* possess equal status to male and female sexes in either the Dominican Republic or Papua New Guinea. Nevertheless, he does argue that by intimating 5-alpha reductase deficiency was a disease to be cured rather than evidence of a third, if rare, sex, the Dominican Republic researchers may have unwittingly destroyed a viable three-sex-with-two-genders system.[34] *Guevedoche* are in fact now quite rare in the Dominican Republic, because doctors diagnose the condition at birth and immediately "correct" it with hormones.

Interestingly, Dreger traces a similar disappearance of those with intersexed conditions in France and England during the early twentieth century.[35] She claims that in the last part of the nineteenth century, both countries experienced an upsurge in the recorded instances of "hermaphrodism." Nevertheless, rather than viewing these individuals as a new or third sex, medical authorities made concerted efforts to erase them, in this case not with hormones but by reclassifying them out of existence.

FROM THREE TO TWO SEXES

Dreger attributes the increase in reports of intersexed conditions or "hermaphrodism" in France and England at the end of the nineteenth century to three factors. First, access to medical care improved, and gynecology emerged as a medical discipline. These developments meant that more doctors with more training were examining more genitalia, and as a result, they were finding more genitalia that did not look the way the doctors thought they should. Second, the number of medical journals and publications increased. Hence, more medical results were reported to more medical professionals; consequently, more cases of hermaphrodism were reported as well. Finally, because more medical professionals were made aware of the existence of hermaphrodism, more were on the lookout for it, and more found it. "Seek and ye are more likely to find, find and ye shall publish, publish and the door is opened," Dreger writes.[36] Indeed, many of those who found hermaphroditic conditions in their patients and who published reports of it became prominent members of the medical community.

During the same time period, changes in the status of women also brought up fears and insecurities about traditional hierarchies. Like their premodern and early modern counterparts, nineteenth-century authorities asked where hermaphrodites fell in regard to what they now called the woman question. If a man had female body parts, should he still be accorded masculine rights and privileges? And if a woman had male body parts, should she be allowed to vote? Could hermaphrodism explain why some women acted like men or wanted the same rights and entitlements as men? And what would happen if a man found that his wife had male body parts? Would he then inadvertently be a homosexual?

In nineteenth and early twentieth century France and England, the response to these questions was to try to make sure they rarely arose. Hermaphrodites might be a theoretical possibility, but in practice, medical authorities maintained, almost all would turn out to be really either men or women. Doctors were to be ever diligent in looking for signs of what might appear to be hermaphroditic conditions. When they found such signs, however, their task was to determine what the condition-holder's "true sex" was—whether, in other words, the person was really male or really female. How were they to make this determination? Dreger claims that from about 1870 to about 1915, the medical community thought the evidence of which sex a hermaphrodite truly was lay in the anatomical character of the gonadal tissue. If that tissue turned out to be ovarian, the hermaphrodite—or actually, the pseudo-hermaphrodite—would really be a woman, and if that tissue turned out to be testicular, the hermaphrodite would really be a man.

Dreger says this solution had at least two problems: First, doctors were often unable to find evidence of either testicles or ovaries, and second, when they could find gonadal tissue, doctors were often unable to diagnose what it was. Exploratory surgery was dangerous in the nineteenth century, and biopsies were not performed on sex glands until the 1910s. At the same time, relying on appearance alone could be misleading. As one expert pointed out, an underdeveloped penis combined with undescended testicles and a rudimentary vagina "simulates the presence of a vulva; hypertrophy of the clitoris simulates hypospadias of a penis; labial ectopia [displacement], the testicles; adherence of the labia majora, the scrotum; [and] non-adherent labia, a divided scrotum."[37] Because of such "simulations," according to Dreger, medical professionals were forced to look to a preponderance of the evidence. All aspects of a person's body considered, did the person betray evidence of being male or evidence of being female? In making these determinations, it bears remarking that doctors seem to have included both characteristics we might continue to find relevant to a determination of sex—namely, "hair, beard, breasts and the development of the hips"—as well as evidence we might more likely impute to gender— namely, the timber of a patient's voice, his or her tastes, aptitudes, habits and instincts and, in one reported case, "the unself-consciousness" of a patient's gaze.[38]

This standard of a preponderance of the evidence may have helped to eradicate hermaphrodite status for those in whom no gonadal tissue could be found as well as for those in whom gonadal tissue could be found but could not be diagnosed. But what about cases in which doctors could find and diagnose gonadal tissue but actually found both testicular and ovarian kinds? Would authorities have to admit the existence of "true hermaphrodites" in these cases? And if so, how many were there? Dreger claims that an influential 1896 article, jointly authored by a physician and a museum curator, offered the means of eliminating hermaphrodite status even in these individuals. According to the article, the only scientifically respectable way to determine whether an individual was a true hermaphrodite, with both testes and ovaries, was to perform a "microscopical examination."[39] Indeed, without evidence of such an examination, no report, past or present, of "true hermaphrodism" could be considered credible.[40] Because medical authorities had not performed such examinations in the past, all historical reports of "true hermaphrodism" could be dismissed—or at the very least, reclassified as reports of pseudo-hermaphrodites who could, and should, have been assigned to either the male or the female sex. Furthermore, because in 1896 medical practitioners were also still unable to perform biopsies on living people, the authors said no one could be sure that any living person was a true hermaphrodite. It followed, then, that the only people who were even possible candidates for true hermaphrodism were corpses on whom someone, for some reason, had thought to do a biopsy. Needless to say, there were few of those.

Eventually, of course, it did become possible to perform biopsies on living patients. What happened to diagnoses of intersexed conditions at this point? In 1911, physicians again changed the definition of true hermaphrodism. They now claimed that for any person to be classified as a true hermaphrodite, not only must that person possess both male and female organs, both sets of sex organs must function as well. In other words, even if a physician could certify through microscopical examination that a person possessed both testes and ovaries, the physician now also had to certify that both could perform the biological functions they were meant to perform. Medical authorities predicted that cases of this sort of double functioning would be rare. Indeed, they predicted that in hermaphrodites, not even a single functioning set was likely. Rather than possessing two sexes, as the definition of true hermaphrodism required, individuals with non-functioning testes and ovaries would possess no sex at all. "Small in number, dead, impotent—what a sorry lot the true hermaphrodites had become!" Dreger writes. "The only true hermaphrodism would exist on a microscope slide after the death or castration of the person from whom the sample came."[41] By 1914, she says, many doctors angled to get rid of the term *hermaphrodism* altogether—not because they found it derogatory or unscientific but rather because they denied that true hermaphrodites existed. There were now, and had always been, just two sexes: males and females.

CONTEMPORARY AMERICA AND THE TWO-SEX MODEL

In the United States, we are the heirs of this view of sex. Advances in medical technology mean that Western doctors need no longer rely on gonadal anatomy in order to diagnose infants born with intersexed conditions. Rather, medical personnel now have at their disposal a series of sophisticated evaluation methods, including karyotyping with X- and Y-specific probe detection, imaging, urinalysis, and the ability to measure

17-hydroxyprogesterone, testosterone, gonadotropins, anti-mullerian hormone, and serum electrolytes. They can also employ a series of medical techniques that allow them to do more than just define hermaphrodism out of existence: At least until very recently, the preferred technique was surgical intervention and hormone treatment to help align the individuals' anatomies and capacities with the existence of two and only two sexes:[42]

In addition to 5-alpha reductase deficiency and congenital adrenal hyperplasia, some of the conditions doctors now consider intersexed include Turner syndrome, in which infants are born with female genitalia but unformed gonads; Klinefelter syndrome, in which they gonads do not develop "properly"; and androgen insensitivity syndrome, in which individuals possess one X and one Y chromosome but are born with female-like genitalia and, at puberty, develop breasts because their bodies cannot "read" or process the testosterone in their bodies.[43] The category of intersex sometimes includes other conditions as well. Clitorises can be too large (over 0.9 centimeters); penises can be too small (under 2.5 centimeters); and infants can be born with hypospadias, in which the urethral opening is not at the tip of the penis.[44]

From the 1950s until 2006, the American Academy of Pediatrics recommended surgery and/or hormones to deal with such conditions. Decisions on which surgical interventions to make were to use two criteria: The choice of interventions was first to look toward the possibility of preserving functionality—or in other words, the ability to reproduce if it existed—and, second, the choice of interventions was to consider appearance—or in other words, the availability of techniques that could create reasonably normal-looking genitalia. If a child would potentially be able to bear children, then no matter how penis-like her clitoris was, physicians were advised to preserve her reproductive function (although perhaps downsizing the overgrown organ so that it looked more like a "normal" clitoris). Intersexed individuals who are genetically XY can often be infertile. Hence, the consideration of functionality in these cases often centered on the penis's ability to function in social situations as a penis is meant to function—or in other words, its ability to penetrate a vagina and allow a boy to urinate from a standing position. If it could function in these ways, physicians were advised to leave it alone. On the other hand, if it was too small for penetration and did not allow standing urination, physicians were advised to consider surgery, cutting off the "micropenis" and raising the affected infant as a girl.[45] Not surprisingly, one of the resources to which the Academy turned in making this recommendation was John Money's research on the malleability of gender in infants up to a certain age.[46] For its part, hypospadias could be treated by taking skin from other parts of the body to create tubes running up the side of the penis and allowing urination from its tip.

Despite the recommendation to preserve function, in practice surgeons often looked only to appearance, performing the operation that was likely to result in the closest approximation to the genitalia of "normal" males and females.[47] Suzanne Kessler describes a case of a potentially fertile genetic female whom doctors nonetheless assigned to the male sex because they were so delighted with her penis; while small, it was exceedingly well formed.[48] Typically, however, assignments based on appearance went the other way. Until fairly recently, surgeons could create a false vagina much more easily, and with a more felicitous outcome, than they could a penis. Hence, medical experts advised, "Because it simpler to construct a vagina than a satisfactory penis, only the infant with a phallus of adequate size should be considered for a male gender assignment."[49] As one surgeon more succinctly put it, "It's easier to poke a hole than to build a pole."[50] Hence, most intersexed infants ended up as girls.

Feminists were understandably affronted by the implication here that a vagina is only an empty hole into which to insert a penis. Equally troubling was the idea, at least in the early days of surgery, that overgrown clitorises should be treated with complete clitorectomies without regard to feeling or sensation. Critics such as Dreger and Kessler, as well as Anne Fausto-Sterling and Cheryl Chase of the Intersex Society of North America, have also pointed to cultural factors that affect surgeries and sex assignments. In the United States, XX infants with congenital adrenal hyperplasia and masculine-appearing genitalia are usually brought up as girls, because they have the potential to bear children. In Saudi Arabia, the preference for male children means they often brought up as boys.[51] The idiosyncrasies of doctors can also play a role in sex determination, because estimations of when a penis is too nice to cut, or a clitoris is too large to be feminine, can obviously vary, as can doctors' views of what looks "normal." Finally, critics stress, surgical interventions are intrusive, painful, often unsuccessful, and usually unnecessary. According to Fausto-Sterling, the medical literature on hypospadias includes more than 300 surgical interventions, many of which involve techniques for repairing problems brought about by previous surgeries. Dreger relates the case of Sven Nicholson, who had three such operations. Afterward, he developed serious urinary tract infections and, for the rest of his life, had to be periodically catheterized; nor did he ever succeed in urinating from the tip of his penis.[52] Additional problems caused by surgical corrections of intersex conditions include anatomically imperfect results, loss of sensation in affected body parts, painful scarring, and recurring infections. People with corrected intersexed conditions also often receive inadequate medical care, because they are unaware of the surgeries they underwent as infants. Moreover, individuals whose original micropenises were cut off often require frequent vaginal dilations just to keep their "poked" holes functional.[53]

In August 2006, the American Academy of Pediatrics reworked parts of its previous policy.[54] In listing considerations to be taken into account when assessing possible treatments for intersexed conditions, the guidelines now include factors beyond determining whether the sex organs are functional, how the genitals appear, and what surgical options may be available. In addition, doctors are meant to take into account the "need for lifelong replacement therapy...views of the families and, sometime, circumstances relating to cultural practices."[55] The Academy insists that those with micropenises are equally satisfied whether they keep their penises and are assigned a male sex or have their penises removed and are assigned a female sex. However, the Academy admits that raising these individuals as males dispenses with the need for surgery and retains the potential for fertility. Hence, it now recommends that micropenises be left alone. Similarly, the Academy now says that clitorises should be reduced only in cases of "severe virilization," and that the creation of what are to pass as vaginas should be delayed until puberty, "when the patient is psychologically motivated and a full partner in the procedure."[56]

Despite reworking its recommendations, however, the Academy still maintains that "initial gender uncertainty is unsettling and stressful for families," where "gender" appears to be used for what is more typically called sex. And the Academy continues to recommend a long list of surgical interventions, including "standard techniques for surgical repair"[57] in the case of hypospadias and removing testes in patients to be raised as girls in order to dispense with the psychological problems the Academy thinks the presence of testes might cause. Moreover, despite acknowledging technical advances in constructing penises, or "poles," it still insists that the "magnitude and complexity"[58] of building a penis should be taken into account and that this considerations may legitimately affect decisions about which sex to assign.

Aside from the necessity for treating some of the real medical problems that congenital adrenal hyperplasia can cause, operations to "correct" intersex anatomies remain medically unnecessary. Because they frequently have the sorts of poor outcomes that Dreger, Kessler, Fausto-Sterling, and Chase point out, why does the Academy still recommend any intervention? The concern with the rights and entitlements of men over women no longer exists after all. Moreover, women have the vote and voice their own social and political opinions. Why, then, should we still be concerned to eliminate hermaphrodites? Some people continue to regard homosexuality as a problem, so they might want to insist on two and only two sexes as a way of identifying and enforcing heterosexuality. Indeed, many theorists regard the enforcement of heterosexuality to be key to recommendations for medical intervention. We must insist that everyone be clearly either male or female so that we can tell whether individuals have appropriate, different-sexed sexual partners. Yet, even if enforcing heterosexuality were a worthy goal, and even if this goal somehow fell within a surgeon's bailiwick, it would surely be difficult to argue that maintaining a two-sex system has worked very well to promote the goal. Homosexuality surely remains as much a part of a two-sex system as it was of a one-sex system. But if enforcing heterosexuality fails to legitimate medical interventions for intersex conditions, should we care whether individuals are unambiguously males or females? To be sure, parents enjoy broadcasting the male or female sex of their newborns to friends and family. But is this momentary thrill really worth sentencing one's child to a lifetime of vaginal dilations?

Whether or not we continue to follow nineteenth and early twentieth century medical practice in limiting the sexes to two, male and female, what shall we say about gender? Must we recognize only two genders?

THIRD AND FOURTH GENDERS

Anthropologists offer us a panoply of genders. One of the more well known other than masculine and feminine is the *berdache* or two-spirit gender, which existed in approximately 150 Native American societies up until the 1920s or 1930s.[59] While the term is usually employed to describe men who took up feminine roles and identities, *berdache* has also been used with regard to about seventy-five Native American societies to describe women who adopted typically masculine roles and identities.

Berdache actually may not be the best term to use for either of these identities because it stems from an Arab word meaning male prostitute—not at all the identity that *berdaches* possessed. Two-spirit is little better, however, because it also applies to contemporary Native American gays and lesbians.[60] To be sure, early European explorers did try to depict *berdaches* as homosexuals, but the wave of *berdache* studies that began in the 1970s maintained that they represented a more complex form of life. We might define gays and lesbians as people who tend to engage in sexual relations with members of their own sex (where sex is defined by similarities in certain body parts). But gays and lesbians do not, or need not, change gender roles or identities. In contrast, *berdaches* took up roles and functions perceived to be those of a different gender, and they also conceived of themselves as a different gender from the one their anatomy would conventionally (at least to contemporary Westerners) suggest. At the same time, although the evidence suggests that most *berdaches* were homosexual as defined by their anatomies and sexual behavior, not all of them were, and it was not a requirement of possessing the identity.[61]

When early European observers refrained from equating *berdaches* with homosexuals, they sometimes insisted that they were simply sissies— men who had shown cowardice on the field of battle and were consequently condemned by their peers to live as women.[62] Here again, however, more recent studies have determined that the *berdache* identity was unrelated to performance in battle. Individuals who were demoted from a warrior role did not always become *berdaches*, and conversely, *berdaches* sometimes participated in warfare. Recent studies also distinguish *berdaches* from two other identities with which they were once associated. *Berdaches* were not, or were not simply, transvestites. Transvestites may dress as an opposite sex, but they need not completely abandon the roles their culture assigns to their gender. *Berdaches* did abandon those roles and, moreover, only sometimes dressed as the opposite sex. In many cultures, in fact, they wore distinctive clothing and special feathers that marked them off from both men and women. *Berdaches* were also different from simply feminine men; nor, in those cultures that had a female version of the identity, were they simply masculine women. Men could be effeminate and women could be masculine while continuing to maintain a masculine and feminine gender identity, respectively. Female *berdaches* were also distinct from another category of women—namely, "warrior" women who transgressed gender roles by engaging in warfare, for example, but who kept their original gender identity as women. It was precisely these feminine or masculine identities that *berdaches* did not retain.

Because of these distinctions in identity, many researchers now understand *berdaches* as a third, mixed gender of man-woman or woman-man, often combining what the cultures conceived of as masculine and feminine attributes but capable incorporating a spectrum of gender blends.[63] Moreover, some researchers think *berdaches* were distinguished less by sexual preference or gender-crossing of any great degree than by occupational and religious characteristics.[64] *Berdaches* in many cultures acted as heads of households and supervised both agricultural and domestic arenas—tending the fields, making pottery, and tanning leather. They could also become medicine men and religious figures and were sometimes thought to possess supernatural sanction.[65] Among Plains cultures, adult males were sometimes drawn to the identity by dreams or visions, which they interpreted as a supernatural summoning to take on the identity. Among the Navajo, *berdaches*, or what the Navajo called *nádleehé*, were nurtured from childhood for the role and enjoyed enormous prestige. In the 1930s, one Navajo elder, asked to think back to the time when *berdaches* were more common in his culture, compared them to Theodore

Roosevelt.[66] Whether or not they always possessed what apparently seemed to the Navajo elder as a reputation for skilled leadership, *berdaches* were well-integrated members of their communities and often especially well-respected members of them as well.

Another third gender can still be found, although in drastically diminishing numbers, in the mountain regions of Montenegro, Macedonia, and Albania.[67] These so-called "sworn virgins" wear men's clothing, carry men's weapons, perform men's jobs, and at least in some cases, receive public recognition as men. Although Mildred Dickemann conceives of these individuals as a subclass of men, René Grémaux emphasizes those characteristics of the identity that he thinks go beyond simple gender crossing.[68] Sworn virgins are worthy of their name. In the cultures where they exist, the value of a woman's life used to be half that of a man—to wit, twelve oxen. The life of a virgin, on the other hand, fully equaled that of a man. Sworn virgins, then, not only adopt a male identity, they also commit themselves to an unmarried, celibate existence, which in the past they could give up only at the cost of being stoned or burned to death. In north Albania, Dickemann says, sworn virgin status occurred at puberty and required the approval of twelve tribal elders as well as the consent of the person's father. Upon receiving both, sworn virgins took up smoking and drinking with men and assumed men's work of herding and hunting.[69]

Grémaux distinguishes two types of sworn virgins: those whose families raised them from a relatively young age as sons and those who, as teenagers, decided to construe themselves as men, often to avoid an unwanted marriage. Grémaux describes one of the former type whose grandmother was so affected by the death of her son that with the approval of the Bishop, she changed her granddaughter's name to Mikas and made him her grandson. For the rest of his life, Mikas was addressed with male pronouns and described by such appellations as husband's brother. Mikas voted, and when he died, he was buried as a man.[70] In other cases, daughters became sons in order to preserve the patriline and household. Tradition generally required widows without sons to return to their natal homes, while those with sons were generally allowed to maintain an independent household. The obvious solution for some widows without sons was to turn one of their daughters into one.[71] Pashe Keqi, one of the forty or so sworn virgins who remain, adopted the identity via this route. Her father was killed in a blood feud when she was twenty, and the family's male heirs were all killed or imprisoned by the Enver Hoxha regime. Becoming a man allowed Pashe to provide for his mother, his four sisters-in-law, and their five children. (Under his leadership the family also avenged his father's death. The man who had killed him was released from prison in 2003 at the age of eighty. Pashe's nephew immediately killed him and was then shot to death himself.[72]

Other cases suggest that sworn virgins were not full men but rather a third gender. Tonë Bikaj became a sworn virgin at the age of nine in order to help her parents whose two infant sons had died. As an adult, Tonë's voice, posture, and way of speaking were indistinguishable from that of the men in the village, and he presided over his sisters' marriages. Yet, when his parents finally had a son, his status changed. Tonë remained a sworn virgin and retained his seat in the male family councils, but when the younger son became an adult, Tonë formally turned the status of head of household over to him.[73] Sworn virgins could also be buried as men, as Mikas was, but were often forbidden the traditional male mourning songs. They were expected to tend to the family property but could not always determine for themselves to whom to bequeath it and although they sometimes participated in interfamilial feuding, the cultural norms was that the other participants were supposed to try to avoid killing them.[74]

Ethnographers highlight yet another gender variation that is attached to yet another sex variation: the *hijras* of northern India. According to Serena Nanda's account,[75] the hijras conceive of themselves as "not men," although there can apparently be different sources of their not being men.[76] Some may be born with intersexed conditions; some are raised as girls until it becomes clear that they are not developing appropriate secondary sex characteristics and/or will not menstruate; others are impotent; and still others, as one explained, "do not have the sexual desires men have."[77] In any case, *hijras* undergo an emasculation procedure that removes their penises and testicles if they have them. Subsequently, they live together; wear their hair long; dress in female clothing, including wrist bangles as well as nose and toe rings; pluck out any facial hairs they may have; and wear red dots on their foreheads, as Hindu women do. They walk in an exaggerated female style, swaying as they go, and carry pots on their hips in the way that women do. In addition, they call each other by female kinship names, such as sister and aunty, renounce (at least in theory) all sexual intercourse, and follow a form of worship centered on Bahuchara Mata, one of the versions of the Mother Goddess celebrated in different parts of India. Their ritual function is to sing and dance at both weddings and celebrations marking the birth of a first son.

While *hijras* do not conceive of themselves as men, they also do not conceive of themselves as women. In their view, women are those who can bear children, and women do not dance in public as the hijras do. "A woman who dances in public for a male audience is considered immoral,"[78] but *hijras* not only dance, they also act in sexually suggestive ways and use coarse speech and gestures, both of which are improper for Hindu women. In fact, despite theoretically renouncing sex, *hijras* are sometimes prostitutes and, in any case, often live in houses of prostitutes. When they work at other sorts of jobs, these usually are either typically male occupations, such as delivering milk, or jobs that can be either men's or women's in India, such as construction work, household work, or cooking. Because *hijras* are neither men nor women, they have an ambiguous role in Indian society. On the one hand, they are sometimes objects of ridicule and abuse. On the other hand, Nanda concludes:

> Where Western culture strenuously attempts to resolve sexual contradictions and ambiguities ... Hinduism appears content to allow opposites to confront each other without resolution...This characteristically Indian ability to tolerate, even embrace, contradictions and variation at the social, cultural and personality levels...provides the context in which the *hijras* cannot only be accommodated, but even granted a measure of power.[79]

GENDER IN CONTEMPORARY AMERICA

What about gender tolerance in the modern West? In a 2000 article, Phyllis Randolph Frye surveys current identities in the transgender community, using "transgender" as

> an umbrella term to include male and female cross dressers, transvestites, female and male impersonators, pre-operative and post-operative transsexuals...transsexuals who choose not to have genital reconstruction, and all persons whose perceived gender and anatomic sex may conflict with gender expression, such as masculine-appearing women and feminine-appearing men.[80]

There are two kinds of transgenders, Frye claims: part-timers and full-timers. The part-timers include cross-dressers and transvestites as well as effeminate males, masculine females, drag queens, heterosexual women who wear nothing but jeans and men's shirts, and "a host of" others.[81] The full-timers make a full transition to a new gender, although not all feel the need for anatomical revisions and surgery. Instead, full-time transgenders in Frye's schema include "pre-ops, non-ops or post-ops."[82] This description of the transgender community reproduces many of the identities we have seen in the historical and anthropological literature: versions of *berdaches*, *hijras*, and Balkan sworn virgins. Yet, it is not clear that we in the contemporary West have done a much better job of accommodating these transgenders than we have of accommodating third sexes.

The *Diagnostic and Statistical Manual of Mental Disorders* is telling in this regard. Characterizing transgenderism as "[a] strong and persistent identification with the opposite gender," "gender dysphoria," and even "gender identity disorder," the manual attributes it to "childhood issues such as the parent-child relationship at an early age and the identification a child is able to make with the parents of the same gender." Additional "disorders" may accompany the condition, according to the manual, "including depression, anxiety, relationship difficulties, and personality disorders." Most chillingly, perhaps, "[t]reatment is likely to be long-term with small gains made on underlying issues … The goals of treatment are not as clear as in other disorders, as same-sex identification may be very difficult to achieve. More achievable goals may include acceptance of assigned gender and resolution of other difficulties such as depression or anxiety."[83]

Surely we can understand the dismay of at least some members of the transgender community at this definition. Suppose we were to substitute religious identity for the gender identity at issue here. Would we then define religious dysphoria or religious identity disorder as a mental disorder and treat it with the goal of acceptance of the religion in which one had been raised and resolution of other difficulties, such as depression or anxiety? Would we not rather let those who want to practice another religion do so, and even mix different religions if they felt they should?

Consider as well the case of Tyra Hunter, a pre-op, non-op, or transvestite in Frye's terminology who died in a car crash because paramedics stopped treating her to make fun of her male genitalia and, when she finally arrived at the hospital, the medical personnel did the same.[84] Or consider Thomas Beatie, a man with a beard who runs a two-ton press for his T-shirt business and gave birth to a baby in June 2008. Beatie was born Tracy Lagondino but began living as a man in his twenties. He took testosterone, had his breasts removed, and switched his sex designation on his passport, driver's license, and birth certificate. In 2003, he got married, and he and his wife decided to have a baby.[85] Because his wife had previously received a hysterectomy for medical reasons, and because Beatie had retained his original internal organs, they decided he would be the one to get pregnant.

In an essay for *The Advocate* before the baby was born, Beattie wrote, "Despite the fact that my belly is growing with a new life inside me, I am stable and confident being the man that I am. In a technical sense, I see myself as my own surrogate, though my gender identity as a male is constant."[86] Some commentators were equally sanguine about the pregnancy and birth. The *New York Times* quoted gender theorists Judith Halberstam and Eve Sedgwick, for example. Halberstam denied that the goal of being a man is necessarily compromised by the retention of one's ovaries, while Sedgwick said, "People experience gender very differently and some have really individual and imaginative uses to make of it. That's an important thing for people to wrap their minds around."[87] Others, however, condemned the pregnancy. In the book Beatie wrote after his daughter's birth, he details the difficulty he had finding medical assistance with the insemination and prenatal treatment.[88] The first doctor he consulted sent Beatie to a clinical psychologist to see if he and his wife were fit to have a baby, then consulted an ethics board before eventually denying treatment, "saying he and his staff felt uncomfortable working with 'someone like me.'"[89] Even after securing a doctor, it took the couple a year to gain access to a cryogenic sperm bank, and Beatie says he had to face the ridicule of receptionists as well as the complete disapproval of his own family. Jeff Jacoby in *The Boston Globe* simply rejects the idea that Beatie is a man and compares the pregnancy to incest and the forced marriages of underage girls. "Those of us for whom gender is not a spectrum of possibilities but a matter of either/or," he writes, "regard the whole situation as profoundly aberrant and detrimental—especially for the baby about to be brought into the world."[90] He concludes. "Headlines notwithstanding, there is no 'pregnant man.' There is only a confused and unsettled woman, who proclaims that surgery, hormones, and clothing made her a man, and is clinging to that fiction even as the baby growing in her womb announces her womanhood to the world."[91] Yet, why should we accept this description rather than Beatie's own account of himself as his own surrogate?

CONCLUSION

Fausto-Sterling once suggested that we replace our current two-sex system with a five-sex system that would comprise not only males and females but also herms (individuals with a preponderance of, but not exclusively, male characteristics), ferms (individuals with a preponderance of, but not exclusively, female characteristics), and merms ("true hermaphrodites").[92] Although she later denied she was serious, the suggestion, at the very least, points to the culturally influenced and perhaps arbitrary character of a two-sex system. In a 2000 article, a group of researchers at Brown University explain that whether one defines sex in terms of the composition of chromosomes and hormones or in terms of the size of genitals, sex differences are clearly quantitative, not qualitative.[93] For this reason, it seems odd to resort to surgery or even medication to maintain a strict, two-sex system that may not reflect the possibilities of biological variation. Premodern and early modern Europe maintained a one-sex system by reinterpreting the facts. Is it better or worse to maintain a two-sex system by changing those facts? As for gender, is it not, at the very least, a bit judgmental to compare the voluntary pregnancy of a transgendered person with the forced marriage of underage girls? Historians, anthropologists, biologists, and a variety of individuals offer us a slew of possible sex and gender constructions: males and imperfect males, males and females, men and women, *guevedoche* and *kwolu-aatmwol* as well as *berdaches*, Balkan sworn virgins, *hijras*, and part-time and full-time transgenders. Most of the latter are originally males with feminine genders who become women with feminine genders or females with masculine genders who become males with masculine genders. But why not pregnant men and "changing-into-male-things" women or merm men and *guevedoche* or penis-at-twelve *hijras*? Indeed, why not make room for the sex and gender possibilities of a Shakespearean comedy performed in its seventeenth-century mode, with men performing women posing as men?

Because we have insisted that there are two and only two sexes, we have either reclassified intersexed individuals as really males or really females and/or have surgically eliminated them completely. Because we have insisted that there are two and only two genders, we have had a difficult time acknowledging the variations in how people experience their own genders and the unique uses people make of them. We erect phobias against possibilities of transgenderism, gawk at it, and/or medically treat it as a disease or "dysphoria." Worse, we often deny legal and medical protection. Laws against gender discrimination often do not cover the transgendered, and transgenders often receive inadequate medical care. Some American states prohibit transgenders from changing their sex designation on their birth certificates or require evidence of irreversible surgery. The federal government allows transgenders to change their sex designation on their passports, but only if they are post-ops or pre-ops who can provide proof that they will undergo genital surgery in the near future.[94]

Perhaps, however, we would do better to conceive of both sex and gender as bell curves rather than as absolutes. While the majority of sex characteristics and gender roles and identities may cluster around a central bulge, those characteristics, roles, and identities that slip down the sides of the bulge need require no sophisticated medical terminology or surgical intervention. We now know enough about human variation, for example, to quit pushing all left-handers to become right-handers. Should we not know enough to do the same for our sex and gender variations? Bring on the merm *berdaches*!

CHAPTER THREE

From Performance to Performatives

In beginning her reflections on the socialization of women with the claim "[o]ne is not born, but rather becomes, a woman,"[1] Simone de Beauvoir suggests that although infants are born with sexes, they must develop genders. She also maintains that this development requires social and cultural education. Against Beauvoir, critics argue that gender is just an expression of biological sex differences. But if so, medical, anthropological, and historical evidence suggests that sex differences do not always allow two and only two genders. The evidence also suggests that sex itself has not always divided into two. For the most part, and until comparatively recently, Western Europe held to the idea of one sex, whereas some other cultures insisted on three. Moreover, while in the contemporary West we may be most comfortable with the combination of a male sex with a masculine gender and a female sex with a feminine one, *berdaches* and other identities suggest a vastly more colorful rainbow of possible sex/gender combinations.

Even if, however, we can define sex as the unchanging biology of the body (not an uncontentious definition, as we shall see), exactly what is gender? In their work, John Money and Anke Ehrhardt define it as a combination of gender role and gender identity[2]—or in other words, a combination of the gender roles one adopts and the way those roles function in one's view of oneself. Of course, this definition is helpful only if we already know what gender is, because the concepts of gender roles and gender identities employ the term. In trying to define gender, we are surely not interested in *all* the roles we assume. Roles as ice cream lovers and airline travelers, for example, usually have little relation to gender—or for that matter, to our deep views of who we are. In conceptualizing gender, we are interested only in the roles and associated self-understandings that comprise our being masculine and feminine. But what are these? When we follow Money and Ehrhardt's line of argument, we seem to zig-zag back and forth between, on the one hand, gender as the definition of our identities and roles as men and women and, on the other hand, identities and roles as men and women as the definition of gender.

Yet, the notion of gender as a role turns out to have interesting theoretical consequences. To call gender a role suggests that we play it, and as in the theater, roles we play can be seen as performances. In this chapter, we begin with this implication of gender roles and look at the way ethnomethodologists formulate the idea. We then turn to developments and revisions of the idea in the work of Kate Bornstein, Sue-Ellen Case, and Judith Butler.

ETHNOMETHODOLOGICAL GENDER

The ethnomethodologists Harold Garfinkel and Robert J. Stoller, in a chapter of Garfinkel's *Studies in Ethnomethodology*, published in 1967, were among the first to consider gender as a performance.[3] As a whole, the book explores background conditions that Garfinkel thinks members of societies take for granted in their social interactions with one another. At issue is what, following Edmund Husserl, Garfinkel calls "the natural attitude."[4] For Husserl, the natural attitude is the belief we unreflectively possess in the existence of an objective world independent of our consciousness of it.[5] Suppose, however, we suspend this belief—or in Husserl's terminology, suppose we "bracket" it. In bracketing it, we do not deny that the objective world exists. Rather, we simply take no position on the question of whether it is really out there or not, and instead, we investigate what we do to make it exist for us *as* an external world. That is, we examine how we produce a division between our consciousness *of* the world and an external world *outside* of that consciousness. How do we separate an objective world from our subjective awareness of it?

Ethnomethodologists ask a similar question, but instead of focusing on how the individual produces the division between objective and subjective worlds in his or her own consciousness, they focus on how groups produce the separation in and through social interactions. How do members of a group produce an external and constant world that is separate from, and endures beyond, the particular situation of the interaction itself? How do we produce reality for one another? In the 1967 chapter called "Passing and the Managed Achievement of Sexual Status in an Intersexed Person, Part I," Garfinkel and Stoller ask this question with regard to the reality of gender—specifically, the feminine gender. In other words, suspending, or bracketing, for the moment the belief in the reality of "normal women,"[6] they investigate how individuals produce that reality for others.

Garfinkel and Stoller had a guide to help them answer this question: a nineteen year-old named Agnes who possessed "feminine body contours and…large, well-developed breasts, coexisting with the normal external genitalia of a male."[7] Agnes considered herself a woman, but because of her genitalia, she was at pains to present herself in such a way that no one would question her objective reality as one. By looking at her conscious and explicit management of a feminine gendered presentation, Garfinkel and Stoller argue, we can illuminate the daily efforts in which we all engage in order to produce this objective reality for each other.[8] Agnes' diligence in creating and maintaining her feminine presentation made her, in Garfinkel and Stoller's view, a "practical methodologist." Because she had to make conscious efforts to render her gender real for others, she, no less than Garfinkel and Stoller, had to figure out how individuals perform or "do" their gender—how, in other words, they perform it for others in daily situations so as to make it an objective fact about who they really are.

Actually, Agnes was engaged in a two-fold performance. She insisted to Garfinkel and Stoller that she was intersexed and that during her adolescence, she had spontaneously started to develop breasts and a female figure. According to the appendix of Garfinkel's book, however, he later discovered that Agnes was taking her mother's estrogen pills because she wanted to be a woman. At least from the point of view of the "natural attitude," then, Agnes was a biological male performing an intersexed person performing a woman. Take that, Shakespeare!

Garfinkel and Stoller conceive of Agnes as an explorer in the ways of "doing gender," and they define gender-passing in individuals like her as "the work of achieving and making secure [one's] rights to live in the elected sex status while providing for the possibility of detection and ruin carried out within the socially structured conditions in which this work occurred."[9] Agnes had to research, think about, and manage her gender presentation so that her gender would not become an object of suspicion. She had to anticipate situations in which her ability to get others to trust in her gender might be compromised, and she had to develop confidence in her capacity to offer credible excuses or explanations of her behavior when these situations occurred. For example, Agnes had to imagine plausible exit strategies if a potential employer asked her to take a physical exam as part of applying for a job, and she had to plan for effective diversions if her boyfriend tried to touch her below her waist. Agnes also needed backup tactics for cases in which those excuses or diversions failed. Garfinkel and Stoller note one such tactic: Agnes often went to the beach with her friends, bringing along either tight underwear or a bathing suit with a skirt. At beaches without private changing rooms, she simply declined to swim and had a reasonable defense: "As she pointed out, one is permitted not to be 'in the mood' to go bathing, though to like very much to sit on the beach."[10] Garfinkel and Stoller think that one of the more illuminating challenges Agnes faced was the absence of an appropriate biography. Agnes had been raised as a boy, and until she left high school, she covered her ample breasts with loose clothing in order to be convincing as a boy. When she decided to live as a girl, she dropped out of school and was privately tutored. Yet, biography turns out to be one of the resources we reliably turn to in order to present ourselves convincingly to others as men or women. We talk about our childhoods and tell stories that clearly identify us as boys and girls. Because Agnes did not have a biography that fit her adult identity as a woman, she often resorted to vague comments, or even outright lies, about her past. At other times, she related those aspects of her biography that fit with her image of a "natural, normal woman." For instance, Agnes emphasized that she had always disliked rough games but had loved baking mud pies for her brother and helping her mother with household chores.

Agnes also capitalized on any learning opportunities that came her way for discovering "how to act like a lady."[11] When her boyfriend's mother taught her how to cook Dutch meals because her son liked them, Agnes used the opportunity to learn how to cook in general. When her boyfriend's mother taught her how to sew, she used this opportunity to learn how to shop and dress the way women did. When her boyfriend told Agnes he disapproved of her sunbathing in the front yard, she took this opportunity to learn how to be appropriately and femininely modest. When he criticized a friend's date for being overly demanding and offering her own opinions, Agnes took that opportunity to learn the proper feminine demeanor of being retiring, quiet, and solicitous of her boyfriend.[12] Although we might wish she had not learned these particular modes of gender performance, Garfinkel and Stoller see in them the conditions of securing one's status as a man or a woman in which all individuals must engage, even if they engage in the performances less consciously and explicitly than Agnes could:

> The scrutiny that she paid to appearances; her concern for adequate motivation, relevance, evidence, and demonstration; her sensitivity to devices of talk, her skill in detecting and managing "tests" were attained as part of her mastery of trivial but necessary social tasks, to secure ordinary rights to live. Agnes was self-consciously equipped to teach normals how normals make sexuality happen in commonplace settings as an obvious, familiar, recognizable, natural and serious matter of fact.[13]

Like those Garfinkel and Stoller call "normals," Agnes was invested in the objective reality of gender, and she saw her conscious performances as outward expressions of her true sex. To be sure, Agnes possessed a penis, but she saw that as simply an extraneous appendage—no different, really, from an unsightly wart.[14] She also went to great lengths to separate herself from transvestites, female impersonators, and others she considered freaks. Nevertheless, while Agnes saw herself as a "normal," Garfinkel and Stoller use her story to answer the question of how our social interactions produce the belief in the reality of men and women (whether or not they have a reality). If one steps back from the reality of gender—as one must, Garfinkel and Stoller imply, in dealing with either the intersexed or transsexuals—one can disclose the constant and active work that gender involves. Gender is not something we possess but rather something we do. Men and women become part of the fabric of a group's reality because they convincingly play the part, and they do so by assiduously managing their performance.

GENDER OUTLAW

In *Gender Outlaw: On Men, Women and the Rest of Us*, which we might call part memoir, part argument, Kate Bornstein moves two steps away from this ethnomethodological starting point.[15] First, whereas Garfinkel and Stoller suspend, or bracket, the question of the objective reality of gender to examine how it is constructed, Bornstein rejects a gendered reality altogether. "There's a...simple way to look at gender," she writes. "Once upon at time, someone drew a line in the sands for a culture and proclaimed...'On this side, you are a man; on the other side you are a woman.'"[16] Second, whereas Agnes claims to have always known herself to be a woman, Bornstein wonders what the content of this kind of knowledge could possibly be. Although, like Agnes, Bornstein sought (and had) an operation to remove her penis and, like Agnes, she transitioned from living as a man to living as a woman, Bornstein did not do either, she says, because she felt like a woman. Nor, on the other hand, did she feel like a man. "It was the absence of a feeling," she writes, "rather than its presence that convinced me to change my gender."[17] In fact, Bornstein asks, "What does a man feel like? What does a woman feel like."[18]

In Bornstein's account, the project of deciphering gender requires more distinctions than the one that Money and Ehrhardt make between gender identity and gender role. The project also requires distinguishing gender assignment, which in the United States is a doctor's decision, Bornstein claims, and gender attribution, which others endow upon us based on the cues we give. In elucidating the latter, Suzanne Kessler and

Wendy McKenna point out that we do not usually have access to people's chromosomes or naked bodies in public. If we want to make decisions about their identity, we rely on gender cues.[19] Bornstein notes there are physical cues, such as body, hair, voice, and skin; behavioral cues, such as manners and deportment; textual cues, such as histories or the biography that Garfinkel and Stoller notice Agnes lacked; evidential cues, such as names on driver's licenses and birth certificates; power cues, such as traits of aggression and ambition; and finally, the cue supplied by sexual orientation. This last, Bornstein maintains, is what motivates male heterosexual transvestites to go on dates with other men, because doing so helps them "pass" as women.

Bornstein regards these cues less as hints to gender identity, however, than as rules—and tyrannical rules at that. The work of managing one's gender presentation, as Agnes does consciously and "normals" do unconsciously, is not only work but, more to the point in Bornstein's view, unnecessary and repressive work. It is unnecessary because it is simply arbitrary. There are many other roles and identities we could adopt, even, Bornstein insists, when focusing on sexual preference. Instead of sorting people according to genital preference, for example, we could sort them according to preferences for certain kinds of sex acts or positions, such as top versus bottom. Gender is repressive, according to Bornstein, for two reasons. First, one *must* present as a gender, and in Western cultures, there are "only two sanctioned gender clubs...If you don't belong to one or the other, you're told in no uncertain terms to sign up fast."[20] Second, signing up as one or the other involves accepting a set of regulations about what one *must* wear and how one *must* behave, look, speak, and walk. Such rules are in effect not only in such places as Saudi Arabia. In the United States, for example, smiling almost continuously and very widely is not simply a feminine cue; in Bornstein's view, it is a feminine rule, as is looking away from, rather than directly at, people when walking down a street or, if one is a young girl in California, making all sentences into questions.

Ultimately, Bornstein decides that trying to abide by such rules is tiring and tiresome. "After thirty-seven years of trying to be a male," she writes, "and over eight years of trying to be a female, I've come to the conclusion that neither is really worth all the trouble."[21] Instead, she adopts the identity of a gender outlaw. To the extent that gender is a set of oppressive attributions, cues, and rules, an obvious response is to transgress those rules. Bornstein's memoir includes three types of transgression. The first consists in adopting an ambiguous gender, one that can range from being "somewhat less than rigidly gendered" to taking up "an entirely non-definable image."[22] A second transgression is what Bornstein calls "gender fluidity," a relation to gender that allows one to take up a vast number of different genders; she mentions *berdaches* and Kodiak Islanders who "would occasionally assign a female gender to a child with a penis, thereby bringing great good luck to her husband and larger dowry to her parents."[23] Bornstein imagines taking up these different genders at different times for different lengths of time and disregarding all gender borders. The third transgression involves adopting no gender whatsoever. In beginning her memoir, Bornstein thus writes, "I identify as neither male nor female and now that my lover is going through his gender change, it turns out I'm neither straight nor gay."[24]

It is worth asking, however, how any of these transgressions is meant to liberate one from the arbitrariness and repressiveness of gender. If the problem with being a man or a woman is that each involves too many unnecessary rules, why should it be easier to be ambiguous, fluid, or nothing? Does one not have to present oneself as ambiguous, and must not one pay attention to the rules in order to flout them? As for adopting different genders at different times, will doing so not also involve taking up all the rules of those genders? Is being a *berdache*, a *hijra*, or a sworn virgin actually any less rule-bound than being a woman? In many Native American societies, *berdaches* wore special clothes and/or distinctive feathers; in other cases, status as a *berdache* had to be verified by supernatural sanction, a vision, or some sort of test.[25] *Hijras*, as well, maintain definite ideas about authentic and inauthentic lives in the gender and associate it with certain traditional roles and activities. In the Balkans, sworn virgins could be stoned to death if they were found to have had sexual relations. Thus, it is far from clear how one can have a fluid gender, and take up different genders, without also abiding by all the gender borders, cues, and regulations those genders entail. Ultimately, those who move between gender possibilities will surely have to attend to even more rules than those who live in just one. Why, then, should moving between genders be any more liberating than settling on one? And being no gender whatever also requires work. As Bornstein herself writes, "I like the idea of being without an identity...but it makes me dizzy, having nowhere to hang my hat."[26]

Bornstein sometimes has yet a fourth reaction to gender, in which she advocates vamping on its rules, blending them and performing them in a consciously rebellious way. "Instead of imagining gender as opposite poles of a two-dimensional line," she writes, "it would be interesting to twirl that line in space, and to spin it through several more dimensions."[27] Twirling that line results, in her view, in camp and drag; her examples are Madonna, Arnold Schwarzenegger, and men dressing as nuns or wearing showgirl cosmetics while roller-skating.[28] (We might add RuPaul.) By flagrantly exaggerating gender rules and making fun of gender presentations— although Bornstein is not sure that Schwarzenegger is having fun—camp and drag perform a number of functions. They violate the rituals of the "straight" worlds. They illuminate "the silliness" and shine "big spotlights on the gender dynamic."[29] They wrest social control away from those who insist on strict gender divisions, and they reshape gender as "a consensual game."[30]

Nevertheless, here again we might want to question Bornstein's analysis. For it is surely unclear that camp and drag always, or even ever, involve the consequences she thinks they do. Whereas Bornstein claims that camp and drag represent models for the playful subversion of gender, is it not equally arguable that they simply reinforce it? Drag may appeal to many audiences not because it subverts gender but rather because it allows men to mimic and make fun of women. Or perhaps it is appealing because those audiences assume the "natural attitude": They know that the individuals acting like women are *really* men, and they marvel at the dramatic flair of their performances. Likewise, as easily as camp exaggerates gender characteristics to the point of silliness, it might just as easily reinforce differences between men and women so that audiences can laugh while nodding knowingly about them. Surely such examples indicate that the playfulness of camp and drag serves as easily to entrench our natural attitude toward gender as it does to subvert it.

Like Bornstein, Judith Butler sometimes looks to camp and drag in trying to find models for a subversive attitude toward gender, but she also admits that not all forms of camp and drag need possess this characteristic. Moreover, rather than seeing gender as simply a performance, she combines the idea with J. L. Austin's conception of a performative.[31]

BUTLER ON GENDER

Following Garfinkel, Stoller, and Bornstein, Butler is interested in the question of how daily interactions of multiple kinds produce a gendered world for the parties to the interaction. Like Garfinkel, Stoller, and Bornstein, she claims daily interactions do so by managing presentations. "In some very key sense," she writes, "One does one's body."[32] Nonetheless, Butler also thinks this idea of doing, or performing, one's body is more than a bit misleading, because it seems to posit a disembodied agent who is somehow inside a body and who moves or "does" it. Neither Garfinkel and Stoller nor Bornstein question this sort of movement or agency. Garfinkel and Stoller consider Agnes, for instance, to be an agent who manages her gender performance and who, by doing so, exposes the strategies all individuals employ as the means of presenting their genders to others. Both Agnes and "normals" are therefore engaged in gender performances; all that distinguishes Agnes is that she consciously plans and thinks through hers. In contrast to the deep seriousness with which Agnes performs her gender, however, Bornstein considers herself to be an agent who plays with different gender performances and thereby tries to expose the theatricality of all gender strategies. Gender outlaws, in her view, show that one can play different genders in different ways and do so seriously, comically, subversively, and so on. Yet, whereas Garfinkel, Stoller, and Bornstein thus assume an actor who manages or plays with gender, Butler does not. For Butler, there is only the performance, and she therefore cites Nietzsche: "There is no 'being' behind doing, effecting, becoming; the doer is merely a fiction added to the deed—the deed is everything."[33]

Although Butler questions the actors "doing gender" that Garfinkel, Stoller, and Bornstein assume, we can also understand Butler's claim as a simple radicalization of theirs. Take, as an illustration, a theatrical performance as Lear in Shakespeare's *King Lear*. Garfinkel, Stoller, and Bornstein suggest that the actor who plays Lear and relies on costumes, actions, words, and gestures to do so is no different than the actor who plays a woman and relies on costumes, actions, words, and gestures to do so. In Butler's schema, however, it makes no sense to separate the actor from the act. There is nothing to Lear apart from the costumes, actions, words, and gestures that create him on the theatrical stage under certain theatrical conventions. Likewise, there is nothing to a man or a woman apart from the costumes, actions, words, and gestures that create him or her on the social and historical stage under certain social and historical conventions. To be sure, we talk about a performance *of* Lear. But Lear himself does not exist except *as* one performance or another. Or if we are simply reading the play, he does not exist except in the text. Similarly, for Butler, men and women do not exist except as performances or the managed presentations that exist in social or shared worlds as genders.

Butler also radicalizes Garfinkel, Stoller, and Bornstein in a second way. For Garfinkel, Stoller, and especially Bornstein, gender has a kind of optional quality. Indeed, in Bornstein's film *Adventures in the Gender Trade*, when a child asks what gender one of the characters is, the character responds, "I don't know. I haven't gotten dressed yet."[34] For Butler, however, gender is not a question of fashion, and it is emphatically not a question of choice. Rather, it is a question of what she calls "subjectivation." The fetus moves from status as a fetus to status as an infant and, at the same moment, moves from being an "it" to being a "she" or a "he." To be a subject at all, then, is to be a gendered subject. Nor is that all; Butler also suggests that gender swallows up sex. It is not just that we attribute sex on the basis of gender cues, at least in public. Rather, we attribute sexes to subjects as the basis for their genders. Why, we can imagine Butler asking, is it more important that one infant has a penis and another has a vagina than that one infant has an innie belly-button and the other has an outie, or that one is born with hair and the other without? The answer is gender. The penis and the vagina have their significance only in relation to a gendered social organization for which they are meant to provide the foundation. We could obviously imagine a society that took the crucial organization of and distinction between bodies in terms other than gender—identifying those with an innie belly-button and brown eyes as X's, for example, and distinguishing them from Y's with outie belly-buttons and blue eyes. And if instead we identify those with vaginas and protruding breasts as females and distinguish them from males with penises and non-protruding breasts, it is for equally social purposes and not ones somehow written into nature. Hence, if men and women have their subsistence in the intersubjective or shared world, as Lear does in the dramatic one, it is also only through this shared social world that sex itself exists. We do not, as Beauvoir would have it, begin with a sex and acquire a gender. Nor, as Money and Ehrhardt would have it, is gender entirely separate from sex. Nor, finally, as Wright and others would have it, is sex the cause of gender. Instead, the space within which we are genders is the very same space within which we are sexes—or as Butler writes, sex "is as culturally constructed as gender."[35]

In the main, Butler develops her radicalization of Garfinkel, Stoller, and Bornstein by way of five theorists: Beauvoir, Luce Irigaray, J. L. Austin, Jacques Derrida, and Michel Foucault. We can reconstruct her position by moving through her commentary on each of these, beginning with Beauvoir's claim that women are the Other of men. As it turns out, this definition raises a problem. For to the extent that we define women as the Other of men, we define them only in relation to men. Yet, if we define them in relation to men, how are they separate from them—or in Beauvoir's language, the Other to them? Luce Irigaray details the logic of this quandary[36]: to define women as the "Other" of men is to articulate their identity within a vocabulary that takes men as its foundation. Men are the One, the being who is fundamentally defined, and women are other than *that*. Nonetheless, if women can be articulated only within a male-centered language, then it is not clear that language can get at their "otherness" at all. They are always, instead, part of the language system expressing the "One." As Irigaray puts this point, "For to speak of or about women may always boil down to, or be understood as, a recuperation of the feminine within a logic that maintains it in repression, censorship, non-recognition."[37]

From this argument, Butler derives two senses in which women are "this sex which is not one," as Irigaray claims.[38] They are the sex that is not one in Beauvoir's sense that they are not the One (men) but the Other, and they are the sex that is not one in the sense that within "a phallogocentric linguistic system,"[39] neither their sex not their gender can be "signified"[40] at all. Instead, they appear only within a closed linguistic system in which the male, masculine "one" is both "the signifier and the signified."[41] The "One" is meant to signify or point to the "Other." Yet, since the Other is only the Other of the One, the One actually signifies or points only to itself. The signifier is also the signified. A vocabulary that signifies women as the Other of men can signify only men, who, as Beauvoir already said in 1949, are "both judge and party to the case."[42]

Butler maintains that the closed nature of a gendered linguistic system brings up questions about a substance-accident metaphysics as a whole. According to this sort of metaphysics, attributes such as eye and hair color are accidental or inessential attributes. They attach to a substance but make no contribution to that substance's being what it is: a rock, a human, or the like. One can be a blue-eyed human being or a brown-eyed human being without impact on one's being a human being. On a substance-accident metaphysics, one is also essentially a subject but only accidentally a masculine or a feminine one. Yet, Butler suggests, if women are the Other of men and can be defined only in terms of them, then gender is not as much an accident as it is a relation. It is not an attribute that a subject possesses but instead an opposition between linguistic terms: masculine versus feminine. Moreover, Butler continues, if gender is a relation between linguistic terms, then perhaps we should wonder how we ought to conceive of the subjects, or substances, to which it is meant to attach. Perhaps there is only the language that articulates the relation between masculine and feminine, and perhaps that language itself posits a substance, a material body to which those terms can fasten. We need to hold, "a certain suspicion towards grammar," Butler suggests.[43] Less succinctly, she writes, "There is no reference to a pure body that is not at the same time a further formation of that body. In this sense, the linguistic capacity to refer to sexed bodies is not denied, but the very meaning of referentiality is altered."[44] Butler continues this claim about referentiality by arguing that

> [t]o "refer" naively or directly to…an extra-discursive object will always require the prior delimitation of the extra-discursive. And insofar as the extra-discursive is delimited, it is formed by the very discourse from which it seeks to free itself. This delimitation…marks a boundary that includes and excludes, that decides, as it were, what will and will not be the stuff of the object to which we then refer.[45]

Sally Haslanger accuses Butler of a fallacy here. It makes sense, Haslanger thinks, to say that discourse establishes the boundaries of our reference to objects and thus that language mediates our access to objects. After all, we have no access to objects except through the linguistic terms we apply to them. We cannot get outside of language to grasp them non-linguistically. Yet, according to Haslanger, Butler takes this insight to mean that discourse establishes the boundaries of the objects themselves to which we refer. Mediations are not the same as full-blown creations or constructions, however. As Haslanger explains, "When I speak to my sister on the phone, our contact is mediated by a complicated phone system, but I still manage to speak to *her*."[46] Moreover, it is precisely through the phone system that Haslanger can speak to her. Likewise, our contact with subjects may be *mediated* by language, but it is quite another matter to claim that these subjects are *created* only through language. For Haslanger, mediation is not a constitution of the subject but rather a mode of access to her. Nevertheless, it is not entirely fair to link Butler's argument for the construction of subjects solely to her claims about language and reference.[47] She also links it to Foucaultian ideas of power, to which we shall come shortly, and to a move from Garfinkel, Stoller, and Bornstein's focus on performances to J. L. Austin's focus on performative speech acts, to which we turn now.

In Austin's account, performative speech acts are utterances such as "the meeting is now open" and "I now pronounce you husband and wife."[48] In each case, and under the right set of conventions, the utterance does something by saying something. In the first case, it starts the ordered discussion of business, and in the second, it performs a marriage. Similarly, if I say, "I promise," I have also done something. I have created an obligation on my part and an expectation on the part of my listener. Performative speech acts thus produce states of affairs, such as marriages, meetings, and obligations. They also create kinds of individuals: members of a meeting, spouses, and promise-givers. Butler argues that acts of gender are similarly performative and produce gendered subjects. Given social conventions, what she terms a "stylized repetition of acts"[49]—or in other words, the routine performances of gender—create a "substantial identity," a woman, in the same way that given the proper setting, certain speech acts create marriages and sets of spouses. The idea of repetition here is important insofar as it refers to what Butler, here borrowing from Derrida, calls "citation."[50] The speech acts that produce spouses, members of a meeting, and so on do what they say both because they are formulas that are repeated in standard ways and because their standard repetition signals the imposition of a norm. The activities and identities now fall under criteria that make them what they are. The performances in which Agnes engages, for example, work to construct a gendered reality because they are similarly "citational." As such, they are not simply performances of "woman," as Garfinkel and Stoller suppose. Instead, they refer us to normative conventions, and by doing so, they construct "woman."

What are the relevant sorts of normative conventions? Butler thinks that one of Austin's prototypical performative speech acts, "I pronounce you husband and wife," indicates his complicity with "a compulsory, legalized heterosexuality that constructs opposite sexed-marriage even as it constructs husbands and wives."[51] Martha Nussbaum has a rather wry response to this claim: "It is usually a mistake to read earth-shaking significance into a philosopher's pedestrian choice of examples."[52] Still, if Austin's example does not necessarily indicate support for heterosexual marriage, Butler's claim is that if we ask what the conventions are under which repeated performative acts produce women (and men), our answer must cite cultural norms that privilege reproductive sexuality. From the point of view of what Husserl and Garfinkel call the "natural attitude," heterosexuality is normal. One is born as a female or a male subject; one adopts the appropriate feminine or masculine gender identity; and one develops the corresponding heterosexual desires. For the natural attitude, other combinations of sex, gender, and desire, such as transgenderism or homosexuality, appear abnormal. Butler, however, thinks the process begins at exactly the opposite end, with a set of cultural norms, laws, and regulations that she calls, following Adrienne Rich, compulsory heterosexuality.[53] As the phrase suggests, compulsory heterosexuality requires subjects to possess desires that have a heterosexual orientation. This in turn requires that it be possible to distinguish between homosexual and heterosexual desires. Accordingly, subjects must be understood, or constructed, as two distinct genders conceived as opposite psychological and culturally demanded unities, where the norm is that the one gender desires the other. Finally, however, gender requires a physical presence and thus organizes the body as a male or female sex. As Butler explains,

> [t]he institution of a compulsory and naturalized heterosexuality requires and regulates gender as a binary relation in which the masculine terms is differentiated from a feminine term, and this differentiation is accomplished through the practices of heterosexual desire. The act of differentiating the two oppositional moments of the binary results in consolidation of each term, the respective internal coherence of sex, gender and desire.[54]

In thinking through the idea of power contained in the concept of compulsory heterosexuality, Butler turns to Foucault. For Foucault, modern forms of power do not reside only in the sovereign power of the state or in strictures imposed by the economy. These forms of power are coercive and external. The medieval sovereign could require one to risk one's life to defend him, and he could incarcerate or kill those who tried to revolt against him. Still, he did not rule one's being from inside, as it were. He (or occasionally she) emerged from time to time to require some sort of service, but he (or occasionally she) did not control one's daily or inner life.[55] According to Foucault, however, modern forms of power flow through individuals' beings. They occur in institutions such as prisons, schools, and hospitals, and they flow through social practices such as social work, medicine, and psychiatry as well as in the scientific and social scientific disciplines and discourses that inform these practices. In all cases, subjects are created: the convict, the schoolboy, the deviant, and the mentally ill. Most famously, perhaps, Foucault claims that the discourses of law and psychiatry create homosexuals and do so only after a certain point late in the nineteenth century. At this time, sodomy changes its status from being one sexual act among other sexual acts to becoming the fundamental result, according to law and psychiatry, of *being* a certain sort of person.[56]

Butler sees compulsory heterosexuality similarly as a productive and a repressive form of power. As do prisons and schools, it structures daily actions and instills forms of self-control that reflect genders and set up distinct sexes as the foundations for those genders. Butler warns against misconstruing Foucault's idea of power as if it were meant to function as a replacement for the acting subject. Neither power nor the subject possess agency in the sense of representing an original source of action. Rather, Butler says, "There is no power that acts but only a reiterated acting that is power."[57] This reiterated acting that is power is what women (and men) and females (and males) are.

Butler's combination of Foucault and J. L. Austin is not uncontroversial. (Of course, what is in sex/gender studies?) Indeed, for many feminists, it raises the question of what the point of feminism is and in what sort of struggles feminism is meant to engage. If Foucaultian power both regulates and creates, if reiterated performative acts construct women as the repressive-creative "citation" of a compulsory heterosexuality, how should we think of the basis for feminism or its goals? To the extent that feminism concentrates on securing rights and creating opportunities for women, from a Butlerian point of view it would seem to start at too late a point. The problem is not that specific structures of power embedded in practices and institutions impose themselves on women from outside, as it were, to deny them rights and opportunities. Rather, the problem is that women are already effects of power, the result of repressive and creative forces that produce them in the form of secondary Others. Far from being embedded only in practices and institutions, power is also embedded in identities as women. Such a result would seem to have a devastating ancillary effect on feminism, however, because it eliminates subjects who can serve as agents of liberation from oppression. Indeed, the process of becoming a *subject* is already a process of becoming *subjected* to power. Yet, insofar as women (and men) are already power, they can hardly rebel against it. In the last part of this chapter, I want to look at Butler's response to this result and then turn to concerns that some feminists still have with her analysis.

RESIGNIFICATION AND ITS CRITICS

In trying to find resources for feminism, or any sort of resistance to the forms of power that "authorize" and "deauthorize" subjects, to use her words,[58] Butler's mix of Austin and Foucault means that she cannot rely on such traditional ideas as speaking truth to power or breaking one's oppressive chains. In her scheme, language is already the language of power. Furthermore, the discourses of the sciences and other authorities construct chains in the very sinews of subjects and, indeed, construct them *as* subjects. What subjects are, then, are deployments of power. There are no subjects outside of power; there are only the repeated and stylized performative acts that cite norms that are both repressive and creative. Where, then, can Butler find resources for opposing power?

Those resources are found, she says, in an instability she thinks informs the very productions of power. To the same extent that a compulsory heterosexuality requires that it be possible to distinguish between homosexuals and heterosexuals, it also defines the two in terms of one another. In other words, the heterosexual exists only insofar as he or she is distinguished, or bounded off, from the homosexual. But then, Butler claims, the homosexual is part of the very definition of heterosexual and, in her words, comes to "haunt" the boundaries between the two "as the persistent possibility of their disruption and rearticulation."[59] We can conceive of the homosexual as existing outside of the clearing where the heterosexual exists. Yet, the clearing is a clearing only because of the outside, because of what limits and defines it as a clearing. This limit can therefore always resignify what the clearing is by overgrowing and encroaching on it. A kind of landgrab is always possible, so the identity of the clearing—and the identity of the heterosexual—is always at risk.

Butler looks to drag, camp, and butch-femme relations as examples of this sort of landgrab, or what she calls resignification. At first glance, butch-femme relations may seem simply to mimic the stereotypes of gender relations. Where, we might ask, is the *re*-signification in a lesbian relationship that merely copies a heterosexual one? One might think these performances are unsatisfactory enough in their heterosexual guise. What is subversive in one lesbian partner mimicking a masculine performance while the other partner mimics a feminine one? Butler's thought here is most easily articulated by going back to one of its sources, an article from

1988 by Sue-Ellen Case entitled "Toward A Butch-Femme Aesthetic." In turn, Case goes back to a famous article by the Freudian psychoanalyst, Joan Riviere, called "Womanliness as a Masquerade."[60] In that article, Riviere describes her treatment of a woman who, in Riviere's view, possesses a "wish for masculinity" (apparently because she presents an academic paper in front of a professional society). The woman tries to suppress her wish by being very feminine—or as Riviere describes it, putting on "a mask of womanliness."[61] Yet, for Riviere, the professional paper is the public exhibition of the woman's possession of her father's castrated penis, and the mask of womanliness is, in fact, womanliness itself. "Genuine womanliness and the 'masquerade' are the same thing."[62] Riviere then uses the masquerade to pinpoint the difference between heterosexual and homosexual women: Whereas the former mask their possession of the penis, the latter openly display it. Case argues that at least some butch-femme roles, most notably those in 1940s and 1950s Greenwich Village bar culture, consciously play out this masquerade and thereby provide a foundation for "agency and self-determination." She continues:

> The butch is the lesbian woman who proudly displays the possession of the penis, while the femme takes on the compensatory masquerade of womanliness. The femme, however, foregrounds her masquerade by playing to a butch, another woman in a role; likewise, the butch exhibits her penis to a woman who is playing the role of compensatory castration. This raises the question of "penis, penis, who's got the penis," because there is no referent in sight; rather, the fictions of penis and castration become ironized and "camped-up"…Thus, these roles qua roles lend agency and self-determination to the historically passive subject, providing her with at least two options for gender identification and with the aid of camp, an irony that allows her perception to be constructed from outside ideology, with a gender role that makes her appear as if she is inside of it.[63]

Playing womanliness to another woman reveals the masquerade as precisely what it is: a masquerade. The same holds for the way drag performances ape the stereotypes of mincing steps or girly style. Agnes, recall, considers drag queens and transvestites to be simply freaks. Yet, if they are, it is because they reveal the masquerade as a masquerade in a socially and culturally unauthorized way. Performances of femininity in one way with one body are socially and culturally legitimate; performances of femininity with a different body and in another way are not. The merit of drag is that it can subvert these authorizations by performing gender in ironic and witty ways, ways that highlight, rather than try to hide, their own lack of social and cultural endorsement. Moreover, in doing so, drag can serve to muddle the difference between different sexes and genders, invading the carefully cleared space of "normal" humans and indicating that any set of authorizations is "open to rearticulation."[64] By performing gender in explicitly vamped up ways, drag appeals to norms of gender but, at the same time, undercuts and redirects them.

The image of RuPaul, who once described his act as "black hooker drag," is a good example of Case's idea, because his performances can be seen as humorously and inventively resignifying coercive sex and gender norms. Case also writes of butch-femme performances, "In recuperating the space of seduction, the butch-femme couple can, through their own agency, move through a field of symbols...playfully inhabiting the camp space of irony and wit...Surely here is a couple the feminist subject might perceive as useful to join."[65] Nevertheless, the problem Case faces here is how to define the spaces to be playfully inhabited. If we return to Butler's language, it would seem that many different "deauthorizations" can be reauthorized and that power can be redeployed and resignified in different ways. RuPaul may be one thing, but what about white supremacist acts? Can they not also seen as redeployments of power in the service of reauthorizing currently deauthorized subjects? RuPaul can wear vampy, slink dresses, and gays and lesbians can march through those the streets of New York City wearing excessive boas, as an in-your-face resignification of norms meant to deauthorize drag queens or gays and lesbians. But does the same hold of neo-Nazis who march through the streets of Skokie, Illinois, wearing tattoos or swastikas? Should we applaud this latter resignification, at least as long as neo-Nazis display some irony and wit? If we ought not applaud the resignification, on what basis should, or can, we distinguish it from a gay pride parade? Moreover, even if we can justify resignifying and redeploying some performances but not others, can we assume that we must resignify and redeploy the former in only one direction? Might we not resignify and redeploy gender performances in ways that make them more rather than less rigid than they are currently? Instead of authorizing different combinations of sex, gender, and desire, might we not further deauthorize them? For instance, might we not once again outlaw sodomy?

Many theorists have raised similar questions. As a preliminary worry, Nancy Fraser notes that the terms redeployment and resignification "privilege linguistic metaphors," and as such, she thinks they are "deeply anti-humanist."[66] Moreover, she notes, Butler speaks in the passive mode of "power's own possibility of being reworked"[67] where we typically speak more actively and with presumptions in favor of individual action, of people's capacities for resistance. Butler is not unaware of this sort of criticism, and she responds to it, albeit somewhat enigmatically, in

The Psychic Life of Power. There, she reiterates that the process of becoming a subject, or "subjectivation," is the same process as subjection, but she insists on a difference between, as it were, power in and power out:

> The notion of power at work in subjection...appears in two incommensurable temporal modalities: first, as what is for the subject always prior, outside of itself, and operative from the start; second, as the willed effect of the subject. This second modality carries at least two sets of meanings: as the willed effect of the subject, subjection is a subordination that the subject brings on itself; yet if subjection produces a subject and a subject is the precondition of agency, then subjection is the account by which a subject becomes the guarantor of its resistance and opposition.[68]

The subject that power constructs is thus apparently capable of exerting its own power, although we might still wonder why its exertion should necessarily be good. For this reason, Fraser still finds "puzzling"[69] the positive connotations that Butler gives to the idea of resignification, because exerting power for a more restrictive conception of gender would presumably be as much of a resignification and redeployment as a less restrictive one. Hence, in using this language, Butler "seems to valorize change for its own sake," Fraser says.[70] Indeed, it would seem not only that we can devise different ways of resignifying, so that we can move as easily to more restrictive performances of gender as we can to less restrictive ones, but also that we might pick different identities to resignify. Accordingly, Nussbaum asks why we should resignify only gendered ones. Why not resignify identities as democrats, for example? If there are those "eager to engage in subversive performances that proclaim the repressiveness of heterosexual gender norms, there are dozens who would like to engage in subversive performances that flout the norms of tax compliance, of non-discrimination, of decent treatment."[71]

In asking which performances to resignify, and in which direction, Fraser and Nussbaum raise the question of justification. We need reasons to support particular resignifications and redeployments, and we need criteria for distinguishing between bad and good ones, just and unjust ones, progressive and regressive ones. Unless an appeal to resignification can show us why, for example, we should praise drag performances and condemn white supremacist ones, it remains unclear why we should find resignification an adequate response to power. "Butler," Fraser writes, "offers no help in thinking about these issues. Nor can she...so long as she fails to integrate critical theoretical considerations into her poststructuralist Foucaultian feminism."[72]

Seyla Benhabib is also concerned about Butler's "deep anti-human-ism." Both she and Nussbaum distinguish between weaker and stronger versions of the claim Butler makes about the relation between power and the subject of action.[73] The stronger version is the "anti-humanist" one Butler herself adopts: There are no subjects prior to power; instead, they are entirely the effects of power and, in particular, of a compulsory het-erosexuality. A weaker version of the claim would simply emphasize that infants are born into a world of existing gendered relations as well as other hierarchies and distributions of power, and they are acculturated into this world by parents, teachers, and the like. To say that infants are born into prevailing structures of power, however, is not to say that they are already entirely constituted by them. For this reason, both Nussbaum and Benhabib suggest individuals retain capacities for action and normative reflection that do not necessarily bring with them the effects of power. Subjects can examine and question the adequacy of the normative struc-tures that frame their lives because, Foucault and Butler notwithstanding, these structures do not entirely compose who they are.

Nussbaum concedes that infants are molded by social and cultural standards of behavior as well as by personal and parental ones. These standards do, indeed, constitute a kind of power, she says. Nevertheless, Nussbaum insists that infants also exhibit "pre-cultural" components of identity, including desires for "food, comfort, cognitive mastery and survival."[74] Benhabib is less certain about the existence of precultural com-ponents of identity, but she argues that Butler's adoption of the stronger, constructed-all-the-way-down thesis begs for a deeper and more sustained analysis of psychosocial developmental processes than what Butler actu-ally provides. At the very least, Benhabib argues, if we want to discover whether there are precultural components of identity, we need to connect philosophical speculation "with other social sciences like socio-linguistics, social interactionist psychology, socialization theory, psychoanalysis, and cultural history, among others."[75]

In *The Psychic Life of Power* Butler tries again to respond to such criti-cisms. In this case, she combines her use of Foucault's conception of power with accounts of work by Louis Althusser, Sigmund Freud, and Jacques Lacan in order to get at the process of internalization by which she thinks power constitutes the subject. Butler does not use these works uncritically; in particular, she thinks that Freud and Lacan display heterosexual biases. At the same time, they allow her to trace concretely what she sees as the subjugating process of becoming a subject. From Althusser, she takes the idea of interpellation: A policeman hails a subject; the subject turns around in the direction of the hailing and, by so doing, accepts its terms. The sub-ject thus identifies himself or herself as what the authority calls him or her.

As such, Butler sees it as "an acceptance of guilt," one that following Freud, she claims the subject accepts in order "to gain a purchase on identity."[76] Yet—here following Lacan—Butler claims that this identification is never exhaustive and, moreover, that it always includes the possibility of misrecognition. Consequently, the hailing allows for a slip of identity and the possibility of resignification.

Butler criticizes psychoanalytic theories that see the unconscious as a site of resistance and revolutionary potential. At the same time, in her view, because the hailing or naming is never exhaustive, and because misrecognition is always possible, the hailing itself creates a psychic remainder, an excess or leftover identification that remains available for resignifying processes. Butler does not explain why hailing creates a psychic remainder. Yet, suppose we say that the psychic remainder is a psychic reminder, a reminder that one is not, or not only, who the authority says one is. If so, our resistance would issue from our recognition that we are at least more than, or possess identities in addition to, those that the present authority gives us. These other identities might themselves be creations of power— indeed, in Butler's account, they presumably would be. Nevertheless, insofar as they reject our reduction to the particular identity with which the particular present authority hails us, we can think of them as a form of resistance.

In her more recent work, Butler also tries to respond to criticisms that she provides no justification for the direction of resignification with which she is clearly sympathetic. The key here, she suggests, is to question the sort of normative principles to which theorists such as Fraser, Benhabib, and Nussbaum implicitly appeal as scaffolds for thinking about social justice and social change. On the one hand, Butler concedes, norms comprise moral principles that direct our aspirations for social justice and social change. In this sense, norms reflect such principles as respect for human dignity and standards of nonviolence. On the other hand, Butler emphasizes, norms are also forms of violence, providing "coercive criteria"[77] that compel individuals to coalesce around an average and to be, as it were, normalized. Butler sees the link between the two senses of norms, as both normative and normalizing, in terms of an opposition between community and exclusion. Norms bind us together; they represent our common aspirations and goals. Conversely, norms also tell us what forms of life do not fit our aspirations and goals and therefore whom to exclude. Applied to gender, norms determine those identities the performance and presentation of which is acceptable because they fit our norms, and they determine those identities the performance and presentation of which is not acceptable because they do not fit our norms. They establish the division between subjects who have the social and cultural legitimacy to live as they do and subjects who do not.

Yet, if norms are both ideals to which we aspire and forms of coercion that oppress us, to what do we appeal in trying to distinguish legitimate from illegitimate forms of life? Butler claims that what "moves" her "is the moment in which a subject—a person, a collective—asserts a right or entitlement to a livable life when no such prior authorization exists, when no clearly enabling convention is in place."[78] She admits that different subjects, persons, and collectives might assert such a right. Here, she contrasts the example of German Nazis to that of anti-apartheid South Africans. Both groups pursued their activities without "enabling" conventions or "prior authorization": anti-apartheid South Africans sought civic and political rights; German Nazis felt entitled to a race-pure Aryan life; and neither waited for prior authorization. If they do not "move" Butler equally, then what is the difference? "It is crucial to ask," she writes, "what forms of community have been created and through what violences and exclusions have they been created."[79] Because the Nazi's promoted exclusion, Butler can condemn them. Because the anti-apartheid movement countered exclusions, she can support it.

It is not clear how this answer is open to Butler, however. Her account of "subjectivation" is based on exclusion. No one becomes a human without excluding the non-human, a man without excluding women, a heterosexual without excluding homosexuals. Indeed, Butler writes, "The construction of gender operates through exclusionary means, such that the human is not only produced over and against the inhuman, but through a set of foreclosures, radical erasures, that are, strictly speaking, refused the possibility of cultural articulation."[80] To be sure, as Fraser points out, there is no reason to accept this zero-sum analysis of becoming human. Yet Butler seems to accept the inevitability of exclusion. Perhaps the violence of an exclusion is the criterion for adjudicating exclusions for her. But what exclusion is not violent?

CONCLUSION

In this chapter, we have been concerned with conceptions of gender for which gender is a performance and/or performative. What interests Garfinkel and Stoller is the way gender is executed in daily life as a way of signaling to others who one takes oneself to be. If Agnes can be seen, at least before her operation and much against her own self-conception, as a man in drag, then what Garfinkel and Stoller shows us is that we are all in drag. Drag may be an exaggerated presentation of gender, but in its exaggerations, it reveals what all gender is—namely, a performance. In taking up the idea of gender as a performance, Bornstein focuses on the fun one can have with it. Just as one can play King Lear in different ways, so, too, can one play gender in different ways: as a serious self-expression, as a campy RuPaul drag routine, or as a medley of different gender exhibitions. Finally, Butler pushes performance in a performative direction by questioning the mode of being of the "one" who is playing King Lear or a specific gender. For Butler, the expressions of gender produce or construct the gendered subject so that talk of a material body, a sex, behind the expressions of gender makes no sense. We have also considered the effect on feminism of this trajectory from performance to performative construction. Butler tries to rescue feminism by turning it into a resignifying subversion of gender norms. Nussbaum remains her harshest critic. For her, Butler transforms feminism from a struggle for equality and opportunity on the part of all women of the world into an "entirely gestural" affair.[81]

Before concluding this chapter, I want to look at the debate between Butler and her critics one more time. Butler asks us to conceive of a feminism that does not take heterosexuality as its norm. If we do not suppose that all women and men are naturally heterosexuals, then we have to question who they are and in what either sex or gender actually consists. A feminism that does not take women as its foundation follows, a feminism that instead performatively questions the precariousness of sex and gender identifications—Nussbaum's "entirely gestural" affair. In contrast, Butler's critics ask us to conceive of a feminism that challenges the bases for existing exclusions. On what grounds are women, gays, lesbians, transsexuals, and so on denied basic rights and equal liberties to live as they desire? Fraser, Benhabib, and Nussbaum all look to principles of fairness, decency, and dignity, and they ground them in Kantian formulations of the Golden Rule. Fraser and Benhabib are partial to formulations that stem from the work of Jürgen Habermas and that ground principles in a rational consensus of all those affected. Nussbaum looks toward John Rawls and the idea of grounding principles in the decisions that parties to an original position would make if they were denied all information about their income, social position, and the like, including, presumably, their gender and sexual orientation. Nevertheless, the point all three make is that we can rationally justify distinctions between warranted and unwarranted resignifications of the status quo and between just and unjust deployments of power. Moreover, making and grounding such distinctions are necessary for any feminism worthy of the name.

Butler is, again, skeptical:

> Do we need to know that, despite our differences, we are all oriented toward the same conception of rational deliberation and justification?

Or do we need precisely to know that the "common" is no longer there for us, if it ever was, and that the capacious and self-limiting approach to difference is not only the task of cultural translation in this day of multiculturalism but the most important way to nonviolence?[82]

Yet, here we might follow the Benhabib-Nussbaum strategy, distinguishing between strong and weak versions of the implied claim that we should take a capacious and self-limiting approach to the normative principles on which we agree. The strong version would state that all appeals to common norms are exclusive—even, or especially, those allegedly justifiable in a universalistic form of rational consensus. In this view, a supposedly rational consensus is inherently oriented to the status quo, to that with which it is already familiar and comfortable; hence, it will always consider as unjustified anything outside of its imaginative scope. The weak version of Butler's claim, however, would simply caution against ethnocentrism and would be perfectly consistent with the views of Fraser, Benhabib, and Nussbaum. In this view, any appeal to what we take as the "common" would have to take a consciously "self-limiting" and humble approach, one that acknowledges we are not omniscient and that other cultures, and other subjects, may well know as much as, or even more than, we do. Rational consensus requires the sort of "capacious" encounter with difference that allows all others to speak, to present their views, and to educate us as much as we educate them. Were Butler to take up the weak version of her anti-normative stance, she and her critics might yet reach agreement, even rational agreement.

CHAPTER FOUR

Gender Intersections and Gender Disintegration

In Chapter Three, we examined Harold Garfinkel and Robert Stoller's account of the way that we produce a gendered world in our social interactions. In their view, we do so by managing our gender performances. Yet, even if we accept this analysis, the social world that contemporary Westerners produce is more than gendered. It is also racialized, class-divided, peopled by individuals of different sexualities, and so on. Indeed, one of the virtues of Judith Butler's work is to ask what feminism looks like if we do not presume the naturalness of heterosexuality. Although our social interactions may construct a world that involves men and women, as Garfinkel and Stoller think, it also constructs a world that other identities populate as well: homosexuals and heterosexuals, blacks, Latinos and Latinas, whites, and middle-class and working class people. Moreover, these identities intersect in different individuals in different ways. Butler emphasizes that we are men and women only because of a compulsory heterosexuality. Other theorists, however, insist that gender is problematic even short of her complex, French philosophy-inspired account. Individuals are never simply women; instead, they are middle-class women or working-class women, Anglo women or Latinas, so-called Third World or First World women, middle-class African-American women or middle-class disabled African-American women. Equally, individuals are never simply men but are working-class men or upper-class men or, more precisely, working class homosexual American men or working-class black heterosexual French men. What effect do these multiple facets of identity have on theories and practices concerned with furthering just and equal social and political relations?

From at least the early 1980s, feminists and scholars have had two concerns about the category of gender and its function in social theory and practice. First, even where they stress the "constructed" status of gender as an identity performed or produced in social interactions, they have worried about a kind of exclusion. It may be, as Fraser insists against Butler, that the construction of heterosexual women does not necessarily "deauthorize" lesbians. Nevertheless, when feminists and scholars refer to women's gender, do they implicitly refer only, or even primarily, to the gender of Western white middle-class heterosexual women? Do they fail to take account in their analyses of women of color, non-Western women, lesbians, or working class women? Second, do feminists and scholars suppose that the interests and concerns possessed by white middle-class heterosexual women stand in for the interests and concerns of all others? Do they suppose that the challenges the former face are also the challenges of the latter?

Sally Haslanger terms these two sets of questions the problem of normativity and the problem of commonality.[1] In the late 1970s and 1980s, these problems led many non-white women in the United States to accuse white women of a form of racism. Perhaps most vocal were the members of the Combahee River Collective, who argued that as black feminists, they were "made constantly and painfully aware of how little effort white women have made to understand and combat their racism, which requires among other things that they have a more than superficial comprehension of race, color, and black history and culture."[2] Even those who were more moderate in their claims pointed to the narrowness in the description of what were meant to be women's issues. For example, so-called feminist concerns with an unequal division of household work and child care seemed quite distant from what Aída Hurtado saw as the concerns of women of color—namely, affirmative action, school desegregation, prison reform, and voter registration. Indeed, whereas white feminists endeavored to raise the veil on the private issue of inequality in the family, women of color were often more interested in protecting a private sphere from the intrusions of over-zealous police officers, punitive social workers, and the like.[3] One prominent theorist exploring differences and exclusions based on race is the legal scholar Kimberle Crenshaw. We begin with the issues she raises.

ALL WOMEN ARE WHITE

Suppose one were interested in calculating rates of domestic violence against African-American wives and girlfriends in various U.S. cities. Because American cities continue to be largely segregated by race, one might decide to use zip codes to begin such an investigation. Yet, according to Crenshaw, one might easily find that both feminists and African-American civil rights advocates had asked their local police departments not to release statistics organized by zip code.[4] The latter would have done so because they feared releasing statistics by zip code would feed stereotypes about violence in African-American communities. Popular imagination already conceives of young African-American men as violent and aggressive, and civil rights activists often fear that releasing statistics on the rate of domestic abuse in African-American neighborhoods will simply reinforce this conception, even if that rate is no higher in these neighborhoods than in others. For their part, local feminists might have asked their police departments not to release the statistics by zip code because they feared publicizing them in this way would detract attention from domestic violence in other neighborhoods. Crenshaw claims that feminists who work on issues of domestic violence are intent on emphasizing the extent to which it happens in middle-class neighborhoods and affects women who otherwise seem to lead successful lives.[5] The result of this emphasis, however, is that studies of domestic violence tend to neglect the abuse suffered by African-American women. In short, civil rights activists ignore violence against African-American women because they are afraid of reinforcing racism against African-American men, while feminists ignore it because they think that making headway on the problem of domestic violence requires stressing that it is a problem affecting white women. Thus, racism is a problem that allegedly affects primarily African-American men, while domestic violence is a problem that allegedly affects primarily white women. African-American women appear in neither account.

Crenshaw claims that even when African-American women do appear in research on violence against women, they do so in a way that reinforces the emphases on black men and white women. As an example, she offers Gary Lafree's *Rape and Criminal Justice: The Social Construction of Sexual Assault.*[6] The part of LaFree's study with which Crenshaw is concerned looks at rape trials in Indianapolis during the 1970s and 80s, and it compares the treatment of African-American men accused of raping white women to the treatment of white men accused of raping African-American women. Not surprisingly, LaFree finds that those accused of raping white women are more likely to be charged with a felony, more likely to receive prison sentences if convicted, more likely to go to state penitentiaries as opposed to jail, and more likely to receive longer prison sentences. What Crenshaw does find surprising, however, is that LaFree's conclusions focus only on discrimination against African-American men; LaFree almost entirely ignores the inequality his study also illustrates between African-American and white women: "The emphasis," Crenshaw writes, "is...consistent with analytical perspectives that view racism primarily in terms of the inequality between men... [W]hite men can rape Black women with relative impunity while Black men cannot do the same with white women."[7] Lafree's purpose in looking at the rape of African-American women is simply to see what doing so reveals about attitudes toward African-American men. Left without comment is the difference in attitudes toward African-American and white women: Raping African-American women does not result in punishments as severe as those for raping white women. Crenshaw says, "By consistently portraying racism in terms of the relative power of Black and white men," LaFree and others succeed in "marginalizing the racist treatment of Black women."[8]

Crenshaw suggests that this marginalization of non-white women in social scientific research has practical consequences. As an example of such consequences, she offers the case of a shelter that denied a battered Latina a place because the woman could not show that she was proficient in English. The shelter's residents were required to attend support sessions, and the intake coordinator said, "They would not be able to have her in the group if she could not communicate."[9] Indeed, the coordinator explained, accepting women who could not communicate with others at the shelter simply "further victimized the victim."[10] To be sure, one might wonder, as Crenshaw does, which would victimize the victim more, being unable to communicate with some others in a safe environment or communicating with some others while wandering the streets and fearing for her life. Yet, perhaps more importantly, one might also wonder why the shelter was not bilingual in the first place. Crenshaw insists that this particular shelter's inability to accommodate non-English speakers illustrates the larger issue. For it reflects how not only the media and the popular imagination but even those trying to deal with problems of domestic violence can frame issues and establish service organizations in ways that fail to recognize or accommodate women of color.

At issue in these two examples is a problem of exclusion. The feminine gender refers to white women; the black race refers to African-American men. Accordingly, when researchers and activists attend to problems of racism, they primarily have in mind the injustices and social disadvantages suffered by African-American men; when they attend to problem of sexism, they primarily have in mind the injustices and social disadvantages suffered by white women. As bell hooks notes, "No other group in America as so had their identity socialized out of existence as have black women."[11] The premise behind this non-existence is that structures of injustice and disadvantage move along only one axis of oppression at a time. One is excluded from full membership in society either because of one's race or because of one's gender, and the possibility that the combination of race and gender makes for a unique kind of oppression is lost from view. What thereby flies below the radar of public concern are the injustices and disadvantages suffered by Latinas, African-American women, and other women of color. The title of a 1982 anthology offers a pithy expression of this state of affairs: *All the Women Are White, All the Blacks Are Men, But Some of Us Are Brave.*[12]

The problem of exclusion is not limited to the 1980s, however. In 2000, Beth E. Richie found that "[v]ictimization of women of color in low-income communities is invisible to the mainstream public, at best. Worse yet, when poor African-American, Latina, Native American women and other women of color are victimized, the problem is cast as something other than a case of gender violence."[13] In 2005, Natalie J. Sokoloff and Ida Dupont noted that interventions by law enforcement into cases of domestic violence in communities of color often leave victims worse off than they were before: bereft of their children because they have been taken away by protective services, or prosecuted themselves for criminal conduct related to their abuse. They concluded, "The failure to address the multiple oppressions of poor women of color jeopardizes the validity and legitimacy of the antiviolence movement."[14]

Nor is this failure to address multiple oppressions limited to U.S. feminist or women's organizations. Trinh T. Minh-ha criticizes the myopia of Western women's organizations and conferences in general insofar as they fail to include Third World women. These organizations often claim they do not know whom to ask and, as Minh-ha points out they just as often fail to see it as their task to discover whom to ask. Minh-ha also criticizes "special" journal issues on Third World women, as if normal women or real women— those not needing a "special" issue—all live in the West or First World.[15] As Chandra Talpade Mohanty explains, the problem with regard to Third World women, or what she prefers to call women of the Third World/South, is not just that Western feminism ignores them. Rather, when Western feminism does include them, it is only for additional examples of women's universal lack of power. In other words, the focus of feminist research "is not on uncovering the material and ideological specificities that constitute a particular group of women as 'powerless' in a particular context. It is, rather, on finding a variety of cases of powerless groups of women to prove the general point that women as a group are powerless."[16]

Mohanty calls this strategy the "add and stir" approach:[17] We begin with a narrative centered on Euro-American women's history and experience, then add in non-Euro-American women's stories almost as if they were simply seasoning. The analysis of women's gender remains largely unaffected, although perhaps a bit spiced up, by research into, say, dowry deaths in India or Indonesian women working at Nike factories. Worse still, dowry deaths and Indonesian Nike workers are meant to represent Indian and Indonesian women in toto, as if in India or Indonesia, women's gender had none of the internal differences that it has in the West. Instead, non-Western women are conceived of monolithically—and typically as victims, whether of male violence, the colonial process, the Arab familial system, the Islamic code, or the economic development process, to name a few. Mohanty claims there is now some awareness that this "add and stir" approach is inadequate to the analysis of race and class in the United States, but she insists there is less awareness about its inadequacies as a way of internationalizing accounts of women's gender. Rather, "since in this paradigm feminism is always/already constructed as Euro-American in origin and development, women's lives and struggles outside this geographical context only serve to confirm or contradict this originary feminist (master) narrative."[18]

Blindness in practical attempts to broaden research about and struggles for women so that they include invisible groups is matched by a similar blindness in feminist theory. As is true of a great deal of the latter, we can trace the issues here back to Beauvoir's *The Second Sex*.

BEAUVOIR'S *SECOND SEX* A SECOND TIME

Beauvoir sometimes recognizes class differences between different groups of women, and she sometimes acknowledges that not all women are French or white. Indeed, as we saw in Chapter One, Beauvior uses differences in race, nationality, and class to account for women's failure (in 1940s France) to join together in any sort of struggle to overcome what she sees as the subjugated position they hold because of their common gender. Rather than risk the privileges they attain by virtue of their association with men, she says, bourgeois women ally themselves with bourgeois men instead of with proletarian women, and white women ally themselves with white men instead of with women of color.[19] In this passage as well as others in *The Second Sex*, Beauvoir seems to recognize that if "one is not born, but rather becomes, a woman," then one not only becomes a particular sort of woman—a white woman, a proletarian woman, and so on—but the particular sort of woman one becomes can militate against any natural allegiance with women in general. The circumstance that a person's nationality, race, and class affect that person's gender means that the former aspects of identity may have more meaning for the person and for his or her social position than the latter.

Nevertheless, in spite of such passages acknowledging the consequences of intersections of gender with nationality, race, and class, Elizabeth Spelman argues that Beauvoir most often neglects them.[20] For instance, in considering women's failure to coalesce as a group in order to fight against their oppression, Beauvoir contrasts them with proletarians, aborigines, blacks, and Jews. Yet, where do black women, aboriginal women, Jewish women, or proletarian women fall in this contrast? Are we to assume that they also fail to fight and, hence, that they behave as women? Is it for this reason that Beauvoir need not mention them independently of women in general? Or are we to assume that they are active in the struggles of their class, race, or nationality and, hence, that when Beauvoir talks about women, she actually means only white middle-class women? Furthermore, in specifying the reasons that women fail to fight against their own subjugation, Beauvoir writes that to "decline to be the Other, to refuse to be a party to the deal—this would be for women to renounce all the advantages conferred upon them by their alliance with the superior caste."[21] But presumably, "the superior caste" consists primarily of white men. If so, black, aboriginal, Jewish, or proletarian women may have a quite different relation to it than white women do. As Hurtado points out, "White women, as a group, are subordinated through seduction, women of Color, as a group through rejection."[22]

Spelman offers other examples of the way that Beauvoir seems to neglect all women other than white women. Beauvoir refers appreciatively to August Bebel's comparison of women and the proletariat in his *Women under Socialism*,[23] as if the collective group known as women never included proletarians and the collective group known as proletarians never included women. Likewise, she applies Hegel's discussion of the relation between master and slave to the relation between men and women, and she compares "Negro"[24] slavery to female slavery. Yet, if antebellum Southern white women could be considered "slaves" in relation to their husbands, they were clearly masters in relation to their African female (and male) slaves. Hence, even if it makes sense to compare the condition of women to "Negro" slavery, we still must ask to what we should compare the condition of female "Negro" slaves. In these and other cases, Spelman writes, Beauvoir "obscures the fact that half of the populations to which she compares women consist of women."[25] Either Beauvoir need not have distinguished these women from white women, in which case we presumably need an account of how the condition of female "Negro" slaves is at all the same as that of their white mistresses, or she should have modified her analysis of women to include differences between women that involve intersections of gender with race and class.

Spelman suggests that Beauvoir fails to follow either path. On the one hand, she recognizes the possibility of differences in the interests and allegiances of women as a result of differences in their race and class. On the other hand, instead of trying to include diverse sorts of women in her analysis, she makes what appears, at least to Spelman, to be an almost conscious decision to exclude all but Western white middle-class women from it. It is as if Beauvoir decided, without saying so, to do an anthropological study of a village—namely, "mid-century Paris," as Judith Oakley points out, in which the women studied, "including herself, are mainly middle-class."[26] As Spelman puts the same point, Beauvoir manifests a "determination to use 'woman' only in reference to those females not subject to racism, anti-Semitism, classism, [and] imperialism."[27]

Not all accounts of Beauvoir's feminism follow Spelman and Oakley here. Toril Moi, for one, argues that Spelman misunderstands statements about women's oppression as statements about women's identity:

> What Beauvoir is saying is that the relationship of men to women may in some ways (not all) be seen as homologous to that of Whites to Blacks, anti-Semites to Jews, the bourgeoisie to the working class. In such a statement there is absolutely no implication that these other groups do not contain women nor that all women are white and non-Jewish.[28]

Yet, ultimately for Beauvoir, it seems that white middle-class women express women's gender in its purest form. Just as it is harder to study the effects of alcoholism in people with other psychological or behavioral problems, Beauvoir's assumption seems to be that it is harder to study either gender or the effects of sexism where problems of racism, anti-Semitism, classism, and imperialism may also be involved. But such an idea assumes not only that Western white middle-class women have no race, ethnicity, class, or country but also that they constitute the norm for all women. At its core, women's gender is what it is for white middle-class women. Likewise, sexism is what happens to white middle-class women, so the quintessential experience of sexism is what happens unless one adds racism, classism, or imperialism to it.

The problem of exclusion that Crenshaw identifies thus leads to the problem of normativity that Haslanger identifies. Discussions of gender not only tend to exclude non-Western, non-white, non-middle-class women, they also tend to allow Western white middle-class women to take over the space thus vacated and then stand in for women in general. For many feminists, a troubling continuing manifestation of this tendency is so-called difference feminism, which stresses general divergences in the identities and attitudes of men and women, attempts to emphasize women's strengths and virtues *as* women, and rejects the idea that they must participate in public life as if they were men, or men in skirts. Critics of difference feminism, however, accuse it of the same inattention to differences among women for which Spelman criticizes Beauvoir. Here, we look at two of the sources of difference feminism in the works of object-relations theorist Nancy Chodorow and psychologist Carol Gilligan.[29]

DIFFERENCE FEMINISM AND FALSE GENERALIZATIONS

According to object-relations psychoanalytic theory, the most important element of early infant development is the relationship between the infant and his or her primary caregiver or caregivers. Infants first experience their primary caregivers as parts of themselves and gradually come to see them as separate beings. When care giving is continuous and stable, the infant is able to develop both a sense of himself or herself as an independent being and a particular sense of who he or she is. Chodorow asks what the consequences are for this sense of self given that in most societies, women still not only bear children but also spend more time than men do with them. What difference does it make that the primary caregivers for both girls and boys are usually women? If infants initially assume that their caregivers are parts of themselves and have interests identical to their own, and if these caregivers are primarily women, then according to Chodorow, children unconsciously come to expect women in general to share their interests. In contrast, children unconsciously expect their fathers to have separate interests from their own. Chodorow elaborates, "Women's early mothering…creates specific conscious and unconscious attitudes or expectations in children. Girls and boys expect and assume women's unique capacities for sacrifice, caring, and mothering…They fantasize more about men, and associate them with idealized virtues and growth."[30]

Women's mothering has deeper consequences as well. Because it is women who typically mother, daughters grow up identifying with their primary caregiver. They do so longer than boys do, and they exclude the father longer. Indeed, if Beauvoir understands a girl's interest in playing with dolls as part of the gender socialization into her role as an object,[31] Chodorow sees it as an expression of a girl's continuing attachment to her mother and to their relationship.[32] This attachment lasts even after a little girl becomes attached to her father. As she grows older and tries to achieve some distance from her mother, the little girl does not completely reject her mother in favor of her father but instead enters into a triadic relationship. Chodorow writes, "A girl's relationship of dependence, attachment and symbiosis to her mother continues…and then her father is simply added."[33]

The same attachment holds for the other side of the relation as well. If children experience their mothers and fathers differently because of their respective primary and distanced relationships to them, mothers also experience their children differently. Chodorow argues that because mothers have been girls, they typically experience their infant daughters as identical with themselves and emphasize this continuity in the way they care for them. In contrast, mothers experience their sons as different from themselves, and they emphasize these differences in the care they give them.

Boys therefore grow into their gender identity by accepting the differentiation from their primary caregiver that their mothers expect of them and, indeed, by aligning themselves with a largely absent father. The opposite holds for girls: They grow into their gender identity in continuity with their primary caregiver. The result is that girls and boys have different experiences of themselves and their relations to others. More specifically,

> [g]rowing girls come to define and experience themselves as continuous with others; their experience of self contains more flexible or permeable ego boundaries. Boys come to define themselves as more separate and distinct, with a greater sense of rigid ego boundaries and differentiation. The basic feminine sense of self is connected to the world; the basic masculine sense of self is separate.[34]

As adults, women tend to value relationships over their own independence and to see themselves in connection with others. Moreover, in keeping with the continuity of their relationship to the primary caregiver, women fear separation and loss. In contrast, men tend to value their autonomy. In keeping with their separation from the primary caregiver, they also fear merging into the infantile intimacy from which they already extracted themselves. As Carol Gilligan restates Chodorow's point, "Males tend to have difficulty with relationships while females tend to have problems with individuation."[35]

In her own influential book *In a Different Voice*, Gilligan uses Chodorow's analysis to elucidate gender differences in moral attitudes. Because women see themselves in connection with others, they tend to exhibit what psychologists traditionally took to be flexible, or even weak, ego boundaries. Whereas adult men seemed to traditional psychologists to be autonomous individuals, capable of acting according to principles they set for themselves, women seemed to be only dependent individuals, incapable or severely limited in their capacities for autonomous ideas and actions. Sigmund Freud went so far as to claim that women could acquire only an inferior sense of justice. Because they could not separate sufficiently from the relationships in which they were enmeshed, women would always be partial to those relationships and unable to see things from an impartial point of view.[36]

As late as the 1960s, Lawrence Kohlberg argued a similar point.[37] Men, he claimed, tend to attain so-called "post-conventional"[38] levels of morality, at which their reasoning about moral issues flows from stable and universally applicable moral principles. Thus, in considering action, they rely either on utilitarian standards, which center on some version of calculating the greatest good for the greatest number, or on forms of Kantian morality, in which moral action involves some version of the Golden Rule, doing unto others as you would have them do unto you. According to Kohlberg, however, women tend to remain tied to "conventional"[39] levels of morality, at which moral reasoning follows the norms and standards of one's community. In particular, he said, women tend to remain at a stage at which "good behavior is that which pleases or helps others and is approved by them...One earns approval by being 'nice.'"[40]

Gilligan rejects this analysis. Women are not malingerers on the route to moral maturity; rather, they progress along an entirely different path. Indeed, if they seem to have an inferior sense of justice, it is because they have a superior sense of care. Gilligan agrees that mature men tend to orient themselves toward a morality of principle, which she calls an ethics of justice. For an ethics of justice, moral predicaments involve conflicts of individual rights, where rights are entitlements to do as one wants as long as one does not interfere with the rights of others to do as they want. The resolution of moral conflicts requires principles such as the greatest good for the greatest number or a version of the Golden Rule that must hold for all, regardless of individual circumstances. In contrast, Gilligan argues, mature women tend to orient themselves toward an ethics of care, where care involves a commitment to one's responsibilities to others. Women do not see moral problems as developing from violations of rights. Rather, they tend to think that moral problems arise when someone fails to respond adequately to a specific situation and to the particular people it involves.[41] It follows, then, that acting morally for women is not simply a matter of following the rules or trying to be "nice," as Kohlberg would have it. Instead, it is a matter of responding to the demands of particular networks of relationship. By emphasizing care and responsiveness, women, Gilligan suggests, exhibit a moral strength that is no less robust and no less significant than man's orientation to equal rights.

Ironically, however, while Chodorow and Gilligan's work provides a foundation for difference feminism, their critics accuse them of failing to speak to *enough* differences. Like Beauvoir, they ignore those that follow from differences in race, class, and nationality and from differences in families and modes of life. To be sure, Patricia Hill Collins partially concedes the relevance to African-American women of the model of care that Chodorow and Gilligan supply. Indeed, she emphasizes the convergences between difference feminism and what she calls "Afrocentric"[42] roots. Thus, she thinks that African-American women are particularly attentive to the needs of others not only because they have grown up as daughters, as Chodorow emphasizes, but also because they have grown up in African-American religious traditions. African-American women, Collins thinks, are sensitive to concrete circumstances for the same two reasons: as part of an orientation to relationships they acquire in being brought up as mothers' daughters and as part of an ethic of personal accountability they acquire in being brought up as African Americans. At the same time, Collins criticizes difference feminism insofar as it neglects different forms that relationships between a mother and daughter can take. For instance, she writes, "Mothers routinely encourage Black daughters to develop skills to confront oppressive conditions. Learning that they will work and that education is a vehicle for advancement can...be seen as ways of enhancing positive self-definitions and self-valuations in Black girls. Emotional strength is essential, but not at the cost of physical survival."[43]

Judith Lorber makes a similar point about relations between mothers and daughters in working-class families, claiming that working-class mothers may impart a set of values to their children quite different from those Gilligan emphasizes: "A working-class daughter and son may be more alike when compared with an upper-class daughter and son than are the daughters and sons in comparison with each other."[44] Likewise, the differences in the sense of self and mothering may be quite different depending on whether one grows up in a middle-class nuclear family, where the mother is responsible for most of the care giving, or in a Chicana/o family with "multiple mothering figures."[45] Oyeronke Oyewumi points out that in many parts of Africa, women can be heads of families, and families can consist of brothers, sisters, sisters-in-law, and all of their children. "Where there are many mothers, many fathers, many 'husbands' of both sexes, it is impossible to present the relationship between mother and child in [Chodorow's] terms."[46]

In sum, even if women's gender identity is bound up with mothering (already a contestable claim), how women mother, whether they mother, what values they impart to their daughters, and how daughters in different social and economic circumstances react to a woman's mothering can vary sharply with race, class, and other factors. Chodorow insists that her work is careful "about what [can] be universalized or generalized in its claims."[47] Likewise, Gilligan often calls an ethics of care a "different voice" in moral theory rather than a voice uniquely, or always, specific to women.[48] Nevertheless, even if their work does not descend to the banality of *Men Are from Mars, Women Are from Venus*,[49] Gilligan and Chodorow's broad generalizations are equally misleading.[50] Ultimately, Chodorow and Gilligan fail to be sufficiently cautious in making claims based on particular social positions and particular developments—namely, those of white middle-class Western women.

RETHINKING GENDER AND FEMINISM

Not surprisingly, this criticism of false generalizations raises problems of its own. On the one hand, the criticism has considerable force. Although

Chodorow and Gilligan claim to elucidate general gender tendencies, in the end, white middle-class Western women and their families become the norm. If daughters in white middle-class Western nuclear families grow up to possess psychologies suited to nurturing, responsive to the situations of others, and deeply relational, we have no reason to assume these psychologies are quintessentially feminine. They might just as easily be quintessentially Western or middle-class. At the very least, the assumption that they are quintessentially feminine ignores the intersections of gender with race, class, nationality, colonialism, and a host of other variables.

On the other hand, these intersections surely complicate the task of exploring the disadvantages that women suffer as women. If we cannot look to somewhat broad categories of gender as an explanation for at least some of the injustices and indignities that certain individuals face, can we understand the systemic nature of discrimination against them? If all struggles for justice and recognition must be specific—for example, the struggles of African-American middle-class women or those of white working-class women—what is to stop the disintegration of any collective action whatsoever? The lists of important intersections with gender and of intersectional oppressions continue to grow; to sexuality, class, race, and nationality, theorists add ethnicity, ability, religion, and age, to mention only a few.[51] The result, Leslie McCall writes, is that "[t]heoretically, eventually all groups will be challenged and fractured in turn."[52] To the fracturing of American women into African-, European-, Asian-, and Hispanic-American women, we shall have to fracture Hispanic-American women into old and young ones, old rich and young rich ones, and so on. The upshot would seem to be that if I face discrimination at work, I must assume that it is either purely personal or that it has to do only with those just like me: white, middle-aged, left-handed, transplanted Easterners with uncertain senses of style. Can I rely on solidarity with no one other than a person whose identity is constructed in just the way mine is? Does all explanation become simply narrative description of my unique circumstances?

Susan Gubar criticizes what she calls "a bad case of critical anorexia" that tries either to slim the category of women down so that it stands for only a particular sort of woman or to starve the category of "women" out of existence altogether.[53] Likewise, theorists such as Susan Bordo, Nancy Hartsock, and Christine Di Stefano find it suspicious that the collective category of "women" begins to disintegrate into blacks, proletarians, aborigines, and the like at just the moment as which the category appears as a subject of research and at which women might seem to be on the way to achieving equal rights and equal recognition with men.[54] As Iris Marion Young points out, "The claim that feminism expresses a distinct politics...asking a unique set of enlightening questions about a distinct axis of social oppression cannot be sustained without some means of conceptualizing women and gender as social structures."[55]

Perhaps we might respond to the apparent disintegration of gender by trying to understand it as a series of family resemblances. We might argue that African-American and Anglo-American women are similarly attentive to others; that Latinas and African-American women are similarly oriented toward family; and that Latinas and Anglo-American women share some other trait or series of traits. Still, it is not clear how this series of linkages constitutes a common gender. It appears closer to the game "Six Degrees of Kevin Bacon," which tries to connect any actor to Kevin Bacon in six steps or less by linking the people with whom that actor has worked progressively back to Bacon. Fortunately, theorists have proposed a variety of ways to deal with the intersections and divisions of gender. Here, we look at no less than five. Two continue down the path of trying to define a useful notion of women's gender, one that can nonetheless encompass difference and avoid the pitfalls to which Beauvoir, Chodorow, and Gilligan succumb. Three attempt instead to articulate a form of feminism that can do without a unified conception of gender. In this case, feminism must simply recognize that women as abstract women, without specific classes, races, nationalities, and the like, do not exist. While feminists taking up these five ways of dealing with gender typically combine them, for clarification purposes we distinguish them here. Moreover, we concentrate on their early formulations, because these are quite clear and remain exemplary both for the forms of feminism they represent and for the combinations in which they are currently employed.

UNIFIED CONCEPTIONS OF GENDER

Young and Sally Haslanger try to construct women's gender in a way that allows for both unity and difference. Young tries to accomplish this task by understanding gender as a series, borrowing the idea of a series from Beauvoir's companion, Jean-Paul Sartre, who contrasts it to a group. For Sartre, a group is a collection of people who consciously undertake a common project together, where the project typically is one best taken up by this sort of group; examples Young gives are international women's conferences and the storming of the Bastille.[56] A series is less organized and not at all self-conscious; here, Young uses the example of people waiting for a bus. As she points out, these people collectively follow certain norms in waiting for a bus: They wait at a bus stop; they typically do not talk to one another; they often stare off into the middle distance. They are united by a common interest in traveling along a certain route, but they have, or need have, no direct relation to one another. Instead, they are related only indirectly, through a relation to the bus. As Young writes, they "do not identify with one another, do not affirm themselves as engaged in a shared enterprise, or identify themselves with common experiences."[57] To be sure, this series of people could become a group were they to start complaining about the length of time they wait for the bus, and they could undertake together some sort of collective protest. Nonetheless, without this move toward collective action, they remain isolated from one another, constrained in common by the norms of waiting for and riding buses but focused on the bus, which Sartre and Young call a practico-inert reality, rather than on each other.

If, however, gender is a series rather than a group, then what is the practico-inert reality to which individuals in the series direct their attention? Young names the heterosexual norms that she, like Butler, claims construct female bodies as female bodies. A compulsory heterosexuality forces us to focus on the features of a body connected to sexual reproduction—vaginas and clitorises, for example, rather than belly buttons—and to connect these features to one another as well as to certain other features—largish breasts, for example. Only by linking such physical features, and by excluding others, can we conceive of particular bodies as female ones. Thus conceptualized, the body is one of the practico-inert realities to which individuals relate themselves as women. Other practico-inert realities that position individuals in the gender series include, according to Young, pronouns, verbal and visual representations, clothes, cosmetics, social spaces, and spaces associated with the sexual division of work and other activities. In each case, these realities describe structures or objects to which individuals relate themselves serially, as they relate themselves to a bus.

Conceiving of gender as a series thus allows for the sense in which women have a commonality, whether as bus-riders or as women, but in which they can also possess striking differences in their relation to the realities that make them part of that series. In this way, Young argues, the idea of a series allows us to consider women's gender a collective unity while at the same time recognizing women's differences. It also allows us to see how women can move easily from mutually disinterested series to organized group in the face of circumstances such as discrimination or domestic violence that provoke collective action. Absent such collective action, however, being a woman is akin to being among those waiting for a bus. Each is "a serial collective defined neither by any common identity nor by a common set of attributes that all individual in the series share." Instead, each "names a set of structural constraints and relations to practico-inert objects that condition action and its meaning."[58]

Young's account of women's gender is somewhat more complicated than it first appears. Given her claims about the heterosexism that constructs female bodies, female human beings must themselves be a series, only indirectly unified by a shared relation to the practico-inert realities of vaginas, breasts, and so on. Individuals are collectively those waiting for a bus to the extent that they relate themselves to a single practico-inert reality—namely, the bus. Individuals are women, however, to the extent that they relate themselves to another series—namely, females—that constructs itself through a relation to the practico-inert realities of certain features of certain bodies. To be a woman, then, is to part of a series, women, that is composed of a relation to another series, females, that is constructed through its relation to a practico-inert reality consisting of links among certain features of a body.

What, however, does it mean to relate oneself to practico-inert realities of certain features of certain bodies? And what does it mean to relate oneself to the outcome of this relation? Can anyone have this relation? Young maintains that the women series "includes all female human beings in the world and others of the past, but how and where we draw the historical lines is an open question."[59] Yet, if being a woman depends upon being part of a series, women, that is a series because of a certain relation to another series, females, that is itself a series because of a relation to the practico-inert realities of certain body parts, then depending on what the relation in question is, these historical lines can surely be quite expansive. In fact, depending on that the relation in question is, we might imagine that more heterosexual men "relate themselves" to certain body parts of the series female than women do. Ultimately, Young seems to solve the problem of the disaggregation of women's gender in just the way that Di Stefano, Bordo, and Hartsock fear. For if everyone can be a woman, then no one really is, and women disappear just as they begin to emerge on the historical stage.

Haslanger's attempt to resolidify conceptions of women and gender begins by actually distinguishing the two. She conceives of both as social positions, where social position means a position in society defined by both the way a person is viewed or treated and the way his or her life is "structured, socially, legally, and economically."[60] The social position that comprises women, however, involves a hierarchy of dominance and subordination, while the social position that comprises gender need not. *Gender*, in other words, is a general term, but *women* is a term bound up with subordination. By the same token, the social position that comprises men is one bound up with dominance. In each case, so-called sex differences serve as physical markers distinguishing men and women.

To be specific, in Haslanger's account, one (whom she calls S) is a woman under, and only under, the following conditions:

i) S is regularly and for the most part observed or imagined to have certain bodily features presumed to be evidence of a female's biological role in reproduction;

ii) that S has these features marks S within the dominant ideology of S's society as someone who ought to occupy certain kinds of social position that are in fact subordinate...and

iii) the fact that S satisfies (i) and (ii) plays a role in S's systematic subordination.[61]

In other words, one is a woman only if people typically see or imagine in one certain physical features that they connect to the ability to bear children and, because of this supposed ability, to a subordinate position in the society. In addition, the supposed ability to bear children and the subordinate position in society contribute to a systematic subordination across all, or at least most, dimensions of one's life.

Haslanger claims two virtues for her account. First, it allows individuals to count as women to the extent that they occupy subordinate positions in a social hierarchy in which these positions are signaled out and justified by reference to the position the individuals are thought to assume in reproduction. Second, the analysis allows for the content of these subordinate positions to differ from culture to culture, from historical era to historical era, as well as from race to race and from class to class. The account thus allows for a dimension in which women share a feature in common—namely, a subordinate social position—and a dimension in which they can differ—namely, in the specific content of that subordination.

For a description of subordination, Haslanger turns back to Young. In the spirit of Foucault, Young ties subordination not to conscious tyrannies or unfair laws but instead "to the vast and deep injustices some groups suffer as a consequence of often unconscious assumptions and reactions of well-meaning people in ordinary interactions, media and cultural stereotypes, and structural features of bureaucratic hierarchies and market mechanisms."[62] Defined in this way, Young specifies five forms of subordination: exploitation, marginalization, powerlessness, cultural imperialism, and systematic violence. For Haslanger, the important point here is that one can be privileged, and even dominant, in some respects while subordinate in others. A white middle-class woman, for example, might be exploited insofar as her husband makes use of her domestic labor and emotional nurturing without reciprocating or even thinking of reciprocating. At the same time, this woman might also be relatively privileged compared to, say, marginalized day laborers, powerless Indonesian factory workers, and poor women subject to daily indignities. Likewise, a black man or other person of color might be dominant in some contexts and subordinate in others. In the latter context, when one is powerless, Haslanger contends that one is functioning as a woman.

Haslanger's definition of women's identity attaches purely negative meanings to it. What is positive, she reserves for the concept of gender, which she defines as consisting of all, and only, those in a particular context (C):

   i) who are regularly observed or imagined to have certain bodily features presumed in C to be evidence of their reproductive capacities;
   ii) whose having (or being imagined to have) these features marks them within the context of the ideology in C as motivating and justifying some aspect(s) of their social position; and
   iii) whose satisfying (i) and (ii) plays (or would play) a role in C in their social position's having one of another of these designated aspects.[63]

In less technical parlance: genders are related to features connected with reproduction, and this connection motivates and justifies at least one aspect of the gender's social position. Thus, although women are always defined negatively, gender is neutral and non-hierarchical. Yet, this separation of gender and women seems to do nothing for the homogeneous account of those gendered as women—here, women as powerless—to which critics of this sort of "false generalization" objected in the first place. Haslanger's definitions solve the problem of various gender intersections by transplanting them from the concept of gender to dimensions of subordination. Yet, if to function as a woman is to be exploited, marginalized, or powerless, or to be subjected to cultural imperialism or systematic violence because of one's perceived role in reproduction, ought we not attend to the specific facets of this definition? And are these not precisely what disconnect women from one another? If I am a woman because my husband systematically beats me, and if you are a woman because you are expected to do the work of caring in the family, what is it that is the same about us? To return to Young's analysis, if I am waiting for the bus because I need to get to work and you are waiting for the bus because you want to get from the airport to a vacation destination, is there really anything the same about us?

GENEALOGICAL, STRATEGIC, AND POSTMODERN FEMINISMS

Rather than trying to rehabilitate a unified conception of women or gender, some theorists try to establish the possibility of a feminism with a disjointed conception. Here we focus on three approaches by Joan Wallach Scott, Denise Riley and Nancy Fraser with Linda Nicholson. To a certain extent, these theorists agree with Julia Kristeva that the only honest feminist position is an entirely negative one, restricting its remarks on gender to "That's not it" and "That's still not it."[64] All three theories also go a bit further, however.

We begin with a genealogical feminism that limits itself to retracing the historical steps by which the identities of women or particular groups of women are constructed. Joan Wallach Scott's analysis of a dispute within the French garment trades during the 1840s is a good example.[65] At the time, manufacturers were beginning to sell increasing numbers of garments as ready-to-wear clothes, cut and sewn in standard sizes. Workers could make such garments outside of tailoring shops, in their own homes, and therefore at a lower cost to their employers. Of course, this development worked against the fortunes of custom tailors. Hence, while employers sought to move more and more work to domestic settings in order to save costs, tailors began to agitate for laws that would require all garment work to be done in shops. Their strategy was to position themselves as "honorable craftsmen," members of a venerable artisan tradition.[66] Tailors, they argued, possessed a special expertise and practiced it in proper business establishments. In contrast, those who sewed garments at home were simply seamstresses, not tailors, and rather than possessing a skill, they merely sewed at night and in their spare time, after their domestic chores were done. For this reason, the tailors argued, taking the garment trade out of proper business establishments and placing it in the home would obscure important distinctions between "day and night, work and rest, parents and children, men and women."[67] Tailoring suited daylight hours, professional shops, and the attention of adults; home-based sewing suited nighttime hours, periods of rest, and a form of attention commensurate with attending to other chores. Tailors were men; seamstresses were women. Tailoring was skilled work; seamstressing was piecemeal work that anyone could do.

Scott claims that the seamstresses tried to challenge these equations. Whereas the tailors' position equated women with a lack of skill and a domestic setting, the seamstresses themselves tried to define women as responsible workers. They insisted that their work was equivalent to the tailoring done in shops and, moreover, that because it was equivalent, they deserved both the pay that men received and the voting rights to which men were entitled. Ultimately, however, the tailors won the dispute, and by winning it, helped to construct both a gendered workforce and a series of associations that helped to define the genders of workingmen and workingwomen. Workingwomen's gender became consistent with unskilled and subsidiary work; workingmen's gender, in contrast, became consistent with skilled and professional work. The associations are mutually reinforcing: Workingwomen's gender is constructed in terms of unskilled subsidiary work, and unskilled subsidiary work is constructed as women's labor. Likewise, workingmen's gender is constructed in terms of skilled important work, just as professional work and out-of-the-home businesses are constructed as masculine. Scott emphasizes the contingent nature of these constructions. Even if skill and professional work became masculine while lack of skills and home-based work became feminine, these developments were never necessary. Instead, they were simply a by-product of the tailors' victory in the fight for their livelihoods.

How does this kind of genealogical approach advance feminist goals and/or the concerns of women? Scott rests her case on genealogy's ability to demonstrate the historical and contested character of the associations we take for granted regarding women and, indeed, on its ability to demonstrate the completely contingent character of the dimensions meant to constitute their identity—or in other words, to construct who women are. Had the conclusion of the fight with the tailors gone the other way, women workers, Scott suggests, would have had a different status and a different identity. Yet, given Scott's strict genealogy, it is not clear that she can conceive of this outcome as better than the actual outcome. French seamstresses struggled against their identification as unskilled subsidiary workers and emphasized their responsibilities in providing for their families, which in their view merited both better pay and the right to vote. Scott sympathizes with their cause. Nevertheless, she gives us no reason to find their struggle more worthy than that of the tailors. Indeed, suppose women's work had been deemed skilled work and their family responsibilities had been seen as sufficient condition for suffrage. From a genealogical point of view, this outcome would have been just as contingent, historical, and contested as the actual result, which suggested that with regard to wage hikes, women's work was unskilled labor and, with regard to suffrage, women's responsibility was to the home, not the vote. Despite Scott's implicit sympathies, then, her genealogical analysis does not offer us any reason to think that one construction of women's identity is better than another: Women can be unskilled laborers whose work in the home precludes political suffrage, or they can be workers with an economic and political worth equal to that of men. Genealogy, however, is limited to highlighting these possibilities and stressing the historical contingency that resulted in one set of identifications rather than another.

Perhaps in part to compensate for this neutrality, Denise Riley argues for supplementing genealogical feminism with strategic feminism, and she obliquely refers to another one of Scott's analyses in order to do so.[68] The question in the case of *Equal Employment Opportunity Commission v. Sears*[69] was whether Sears actively discriminated against women by failing to promote or hire them into commission sales positions. Workers in these positions sold "big-ticket" items, such as tires and fencing, and they usually earned more than those in non-commission sales positions. Although the case had no actual plaintiffs, the statistical evidence the Equal Employment Opportunity Commission gathered indicated that very few women occupied positions in commission sales. The question was, then, what did these low numbers indicate?

Opposing feminist offered different analyses. Serving as an expert witness for Sears, Rosalind Rosenberg adopted a Chodorow-Gilligan-type thesis and testified that the statistics indicated only women's own preferences. Women, historically, have held different goals and interests with regard to work, Rosenberg claimed. They have preferred to sell softer products like clothing and housewares, which at Sears were sold on a non-commission basis. Moreover, because household obligations and child care responsibilities affected women's labor, "many women choose jobs that complement their family obligations over jobs that might increase and enhance their earning potential."[70] Because commission sales often involve full-time work, weekend work, and irregular hours, women, according to Rosenberg, tended to avoid it.

Alice Kessler-Harris, serving as an expert witness for the government, argued that women's job choices were more complex. In her view, these choices should be understood as a combination of culturally acceptable interests, self-perceptions, and the positions made available to women. If certain positions such as selling tires were considered to be outside the culturally accepted boundaries for women's work, then the low presence of women in those positions said very little about what their job preferences might be in the absence of these boundaries. Indeed, Kessler-Harris argued, whenever positions previously outside such boundaries did become available, women generally took them. For example, when positions in real estate, insurance, and banking became open to women in the 1920s, women took and held on to them until the Great Depression, when cultural pressures and economic prejudices again worked to reserve these positions for men. During both World Wars, women left lower-paying jobs to take the higher-paying positions as welders, shop-fitters, and crane operators that became vacant when men joined the armed services. In the 1960s and 1970s, women also quickly became lawyers, businesswomen, and doctors as soon as such positions were no longer outside socially acceptable boundaries for them. According to Kessler-Harris, such facts "suggest that ideas about women's traditional roles are neither deeply rooted in women's psyche nor do they form a barrier that inhibits women's work force participation."[71] In her view, then, the low numbers of women in commission sales at Sears were most likely the result of a company prejudice against hiring women to fill them.

What are we to make of these opposing feminist testimonies? Riley suggests that both make some sense. On the one hand, feminists can plausibly argue that women workers have different employment interests from men because of women's commitments to their families and roles as wives and mothers—in short because of their identities as Chodorow and Gilligan's selves-in-relation. On the other hand, feminists can equally easily argue the opposite: Women workers are just as interested in increasing their pay as men are, and they are willing to take positions with greater risks and responsibilities in order to do so. Riley actually thinks that both arguments are awkward insofar as they leave the impression that women workers are a group—and a monolithic group at that—with a unified set of gender-defined interests. At the same time, she insists that because, when merged together, the positions argue that women workers are both the same as and different from male workers, they "effectively mudd[y] that term [women workers]."[72] In other words, if women workers both pursue and diverge from a male career path, it follows that by focusing on women in trying to explain work-force statistics, we are focusing on a nonexistent, disaggregated collective. Moreover, she asserts, this recognition of its nonexistence—or at least, muddiness—forms the substance of feminism: "That 'women' is indeterminate and impossible is no cause for lament. It is what makes feminism; which has hardly been an indiscriminate embrace anyway of the fragilities and peculiarities of the category."[73]

Still, if it is hard to see how Scott's genealogy gives us reasons to cheer for one side or the other in the garment wars, it is also difficult to envision what a feminist practice that embraces the indeterminacy and impossibility of gendered collectives might look like. Would this not be to embrace the indeterminacy and impossibility of feminism's own rationale? If women's gender is a fragile, and even impossible, tool for analyzing data, institutions, structures, or the like, why use it at all? Ultimately, Riley claims feminists must be strategic. Feminists must recognize "that it is compatible to suggest that 'women' don't exist—while maintaining a politics of 'as if they existed'—since the world behaves as if they unambiguously did."[74] In other words, feminism must recognize that women do not form a homogenous collective gender with a unified conception of legal and political issues while maintaining for strategic reasons—in other words, when it is in the interests of feminism to do so—that they do. Yet, for Riley, the initial spur for rethinking feminism is the recognition that women do not form a homogenous gender. Ought she therefore not also recognize that different women or groups of women may differ on whether and when they think an "as if" politics is in their interests? Given both the heterogeneity of women and the constructions of women that Riley emphasizes, how can she anticipate agreement on the circumstances and causes for which they will agree to be "women" for strategic purposes?

In their own attempt to find a form of feminism that is compatible with tensions within the category of gender, Fraser and Nicholson offer what they call a "postmodern" feminist theory comprising four features.[75] First, it is, as Scott would agree, "explicitly historical, attuned to the cultural specificity of different societies and periods and to that of different groups within societies and periods."[76] Second, where a postmodern feminist theory focuses on phenomena that seem to cross cultures, it restricts itself to making comparisons between the phenomena. Third, postmodern feminist theory is pragmatic and pluralistic, tailoring "its methods and categories to the specific task at hand, using multiple categories when appropriate and forswearing the metaphysical comfort of a single feminist method."[77] Finally, it replaces "unitary notions of woman and feminine gender identity with plural and complexly structured conceptions of social identity, treating gender as one relevant strand among others, attending also to class, race, ethnicity, age and sexual orientation."[78] Fraser and Nicholson suggest that one merit of this sort of theory is that it supports current feminist practice, which they find "increasingly a matter of alliances rather than one of unity around a universally shared interest or identity." They continue:

> It recognizes that the diversity of women's needs and experiences means that no single solution, on issues like child care, social security, and housing, can be adequate for all...The underlying premise of this practice is that, while some women share some common interests and face some common enemies, such commonalities are by no means universal; rather they are interlaced with differences, even with conflicts.[79]

Fraser and Nicholson taken an obviously Eurocentric focus in neglecting religion and nationality and singling out only class, race, ethnicity, age, and sexual orientation as the characteristics to which feminists ought to attend. Nevertheless, and despite Mohanty's own contempt for the category of postmodernism, the first two features of this analysis fit well with what she calls a decolonizing feminism or a comparative feminist studies model. In her version, the model attends first to local processes and socioeconomic groups, then moves toward comparisons between situations that show the way in which groups of women are reciprocally constituted. For instance, we might explore the "interconnections between the history, experiences, and struggles of U.S. women of color, white women, and women from the Third World/South."[80] The focus, however, is not simply on intersections of gender with race, class, or nationality within different communities.

Rather, Mohanty stresses, "mutuality and coimplication."[81] In other words, we look for the ways in which the identity of, say, white Western women is constructed through and in relation to the construction of the identity of colonial women, and vice versa; likewise, we look for the ways that African-American women are constructed through and in relation to the construction of Euro-American women, and vice versa; and so on. In this way, Mohanty's model allows for comparisons without overarching narratives and for co-implication, or co-construction, so that Euro-American women no longer serve as the self-sufficient norm of womanhood to which we simply add and stir in others.

So far, so good. The second two features of Fraser and Nicholson's account are more problematic, however. Like Riley, Fraser and Nicholson are unbothered by the differences, and even conflicts, both within and about the commonalities that are meant to constitute women's gender. Instead, they think that feminist theory ought simply to follow feminist practice in recognizing them. In fact, Fraser and Nicholson go Riley one better. Riley acknowledges differences and conflicts in the gender category of women. But she thinks they can be overcome in a strategic politics that proceeds as if women existed. In contrast, Fraser and Nicholson allow for conflicts and differences within feminist practice itself. But surely at least some differences and conflicts must be disturbing for that practice. For example, one solution to the absence of sufficient and adequate child care for a group of women workers might be to build child care facilities on company grounds. But suppose doing so leads to further exploitation of women at the company's plants in, say, Indonesia? It is one thing to recognize that different women may need different solutions to such issues as balancing work and childcare or exploitation and starvation; it is another to think feminist practice need not resolve these conflicts. If the commonalities that some women share "are by no means universal," and if even these "are interlaced with differences, even with conflicts," it is difficult to think we can stop there, without a consensus on either our principles or our strategies.

CONCLUSION

For the theorists we have looked at in this chapter, gender never appears in a pure state; it is always, at the very least, raced and classed and often colonized. These modulations are devastating to its unity. When we try to study gender, we can study only raced gender, classed gender, aged gender, or a variety of other forms of gender. By the same token, however, race and class never appear in a pure state. They always possess gender, age, and sexuality, as well as countless other individualizing traits. Race is classed and gendered; class is raced and gendered; age is raced, gendered, and classed; and so on. How, then, we might ask, is any form of general knowledge about people in society possible? Is every individual so unique and composed of such different factors that only individual descriptions of individual situations are, in the end, possible? Feminists offer provocative suggestions, from re-establishing feminism on the basis of the non-existence of women to re-establishing women as those general and abstract beings who are victims of oppression. Ultimately, however, none of these suggestions is unproblematic. We pursue the issue further in the next chapter.

CHAPTER FIVE

Sex and Gender in Context

Criticisms of what we might call a Eurocentric white feminism begin with the way it overlooks racial and class differences between women and assumes that what holds for Anglo-Euro white women holds for all women. Additional criticisms point to the neglect of other features of identity, including sexuality, nationality, disability, and age. Critics also wonder how we should think about gender in general if it seems to disaggregate into so many particular splinters, and they wonder how feminism ought to proceed—namely, with or without the category of women. Certainly, if research about women and struggles on behalf of women cannot take the category of women for granted, and if theory and practice must attend to location, nationality, class, race, age, and a host of other specifics, it becomes less clear what an analysis focused on gender actually contributes to the practical or theoretical examinations for which it is meant to pack a punch.

We can raise the same concern for analyses focusing on sex differences. In the first place, the original distinction between sex and gender was already meant to absolve sex of any blame for causing women's position in society; hence, the distinction would also seem to make sex irrelevant to practical and theoretical explorations of sexism. In the second place, some theorists insist that sex is nothing but gender, a way of dividing human beings for purposes of a reproductive sexuality. But if sex is nothing but gender, and if gender disintegrates into class, nationality, race, and so on then, once again, we have to ask how attention to gender is meant to help in providing theoretical foundations for women's rights and struggles.

In this chapter, I suggest an approach to sex and gender that is indebted to the German tradition of textual hermeneutics. Linda Martín Alcoff points us in a helpful direction in using Hans-Georg Gadamer's version of this tradition as one of her guides in her book *Visible Identities: Race, Gender, and the Self.* We begin with her analysis of Gadamer's conception of interpretive horizons.

ALCOFF'S HERMENEUTICS

Alcoff refers us to Gadamer's conception of interpretive horizons as a way of illuminating our lived experience of, responses to, and reasoning about our world.[1] Our lives are situated ones. Alcoff stresses that they are socially positioned and take place within particular cultures and historical traditions. We grow up in a certain place, at a certain time, within a certain culture, and within a particular social stratum. As we come to understand our world and its various practices, institutions, stories, histories, and so on, we imbibe the conceptions and presuppositions of those who raise and socialize us. We use their language and, at least initially, adopt their orientations and their conceptions of what is and is not important. These give us our beginning perspective or horizon on our world. Alcoff thus defines horizons as "the framing assumptions we bring with us to perception and understanding, the congealed experiences that become premises by which we strive to make sense of the world, the range of concepts and categories of description that we have at our disposal."[2]

While Gadamer most often stresses the common historical threads that bind us to our traditions and provide the lens through which we first approach the world in which we live, Alcoff uses the concept of horizons to highlight differences in the experiences, perceptions, and perspectives of differently socially positioned individuals:

> Just as a servant has a different experience, perception, and perspective of the queen's castle, knowing intimately its back passageways, its pantries and cupboards, and viewing its fine rooms and furnishings primarily in terms of their degree of required maintenance, so the queen herself will have a different experience, perception, and perspective, perhaps having little knowledge of the underground rooms and no awareness of what her requests cost the servants in work time; she views her fine rooms and furnishings in terms of their ability to hold large numbers of guests, to provide her with comfort, or to please her aesthetic senses.[3]

Thus, what the queen sees as a beautiful tableau to present to her numerous guests, the servant sees as a repository for dirt. While the queen expects comfort and entertainment, the servant anticipates cleaning.

Alcoff does not think that an emphasis on these different horizons leads to what she calls a "dysfunctional"[4] relativism, by which she means a position that views the queen's and servant's perspective—or any two perspectives—as equally valid. In the first place, there is no alternative to a horizonal understanding. We cannot contrast a horizonal understanding to a neutral or objective one, because there is none: All understandings are oriented in particular ways and issue from particular "framing assumptions."[5] We cannot somehow float above our horizons, viewing everything at once and without a perspective or slant on it. In the second place, our own horizon allows us to note the differences between, and the limitations of, other perspectives, and we can link their relative value to our own particular projects. "For emancipatory and egalitarian projects," Alcoff insists, "clearly the servant's horizon will be most valuable."[6] Finally, however, and perhaps most importantly, according to Alcoff, the notion of a dysfunctional relativism supposes that different horizons are incommensurable—or in other words, that they are held by different individuals or groups who can possess absolutely no overlap in the ways they understand. We may see a particular figure as either a duck or a rabbit, but we cannot see it as both at once. The images do not overlap. If those who see it as a duck cannot see it as a rabbit, then those who see it as a rabbit but cannot see it as a duck would seem to have nothing to say to them. Indeed, the two groups would appear to have no way to reach a consensus about what the image is. Likewise, if the queen sees a beautiful tableau and the servant a repository for dirt, how will they communicate or come to a consensus about the castle? Will we all not live in our own worlds, hemmed in by the limits of our own horizons and unable to see what those who occupy other horizons see?

Alcoff thinks this worry about incommensurability is overblown. As a case in point, she cites what she calls "perhaps the most dramatic clash of lifeworlds"[7] or cultures and their framing assumptions—namely, the sixteenth-century encounter between the Spanish and Mesoamericans. Even in this instance, she argues, the two groups shared more than we might think, including "a tradition of literacy, theocratic governance systems, and rigidly hierarchical and collectivized forms of social life."[8] They also shared experiences with cross-cultural relationships and in productively negotiating religious, cultural, and linguistic differences with others. Nor were the Spanish unfamiliar with visible differences in appearance. In short, even in this extreme case, Alcoff sees grounds for mutual understanding—or at the very least, for a productive conversation. What undermined these grounds, she claims, were not incommensurable horizons but rather the Spaniards' greed and dedicated effort *not* to understand. We still need proof, then, that horizons are ever really incommensurable. Instead, they seem to overlap in ways that provide, at the very least, a foundation for conversation, if not agreement. Gadamer has a particularly apt way of putting this point: "Language always forestalls any objection to its jurisdiction."[9]

Yet, despite what she considers its usefulness in illuminating the relation between horizons and understandings, Alcoff thinks that Gadamer's account of the former needs better anchoring. In her view, Gadamer conceives of horizons in overly abstract terms, and he neglects the extent to which they represent "a locatedness that, in reality, is a metaphor for the body."[10] Our historically, culturally, and socially influenced orientations may allow us to understand the objects of our experience as we do, but Alcoff insists that our bodies—the way they move through space, relate to objects in space, and so on—are also critical. Indeed, she says, the knowledge of our world that our bodies contain is reflected in the very expressions we use to describe that world. For example, we describe an increase in amount as rising or going up, as in "prices rose," and a decrease as going down or falling, as in "employment fell by such and such a percent." The same holds for descriptions of our minds. We describe thinking as seeing, ideas as locations (as in "points of view"), and communicating ideas as moving objects (as in "putting ideas in our heads"). In other words, bodily experiences establish horizons just as traditions and cultures do.

Moreover, like traditions and cultures, bodies and bodily experiences differ. Well-versed with the problems we have surveyed in this book regarding attempts to distinguish sex and gender and to define gender, Alcoff uses the latter concept to designate both physical-biological factors in our lived experience, which we have been calling sex, and culturally conditioned ones, which we have been calling gender. Thus, Alcoff maintains that sources for differences in our bodily experiences are complex. They include cultural practices promoting differences in the ways that men and women move—in the United States, for example, men move expansively and women less so—and in the ways they sit, stand, run, speak, and throw a ball. Because of their differences in physical strength, men and women also approach the same task differently, using different parts of their bodies to do the same things. Finally, according to Alcoff, women's bodily experiences, but not men's, include the "experience of breasts, menses, lactation and pregnancy."[11] Alcoff insists these differences reflect "a perceptual orientation and a conceptual mapping that determines value, relevance, and imaginable possibilities."[12] The horizon on the world and her life that a girl possesses when she knows she can become pregnant and can both bear and nurse a child is necessarily different from the horizon possessed by a boy who knows that he cannot.

Alcoff does not minimize the extent to which gendered (in her sense) horizons vary according to the traditions and cultures of which they are a part; nor does she deny that horizons also vary according to their intersections with other factors, such as race and class. To this extent, she concedes the consequences of intersectionality and does not suppose that all women, regardless of their social, cultural, and historical situation, understand the meanings of their experiences in the same way. At the same time, she argues, "The possibility of pregnancy, childbirth, nursing, and in many societies, rape are parts of females' horizons...and they exist there because of the ways we are embodied."[13] We can agree, in other words, that gender horizons intersect in different ways with horizons of race, class, and the like. Nonetheless, the former remain "fundamental to ourselves as knowing, feeling, and acting subjects," and they "operate as epistemological perspectives...from which certain aspects or layers are made visible." Alcoff continues:

> In stratified societies, differently identified individuals do not have the same access to points of view or perceptual planes of observation or the same embodied knowledge. The queen may freely walk in the servants' quarters, but she will not view them in the same way as the servants do. Two individuals may participate in the same event, but different aspects of that event will be perceptible to different people. Social identity operates, then, as a rough and fallible but useful indicator of differences in perceptual access. This argument does not rely on a uniformity of opinion within an identity group but on a claim about what aspects of reality are more or less easily accessible to an identity group.[14]

Alcoff thinks her reflections should lead us to extend the hermeneutic conception of horizons to encompass not only socially, culturally, and historically situated identities but also embodied ones. An isolated street simply looks quite different to a man than it does to a woman. For the former, it may signal nothing in particular, while for the latter, it typically and rather immediately means danger. To this extent, horizons are gendered, Alcoff thinks, and as common embodied points of access to meanings, these horizons reflect a basis for solidarity among women in spite of any differences women may have from one another. To be sure, gendered horizons remain complexly related to race, class, nationality, and a host of other situations. Nonetheless, they establish ways of obtaining access to meanings that speak to certain common and gendered perceptions.

Alcoff focuses on the way in which gendered horizons open up the world for us in particular ways and thus are crucial to our lived experience of that world, no matter how intertwined they are with the other horizons we inhabit. In what follows, I want to turn her analysis around. Suppose we ask not how gender horizons allow us to see or understand but what we understand of them?

TEXTUAL UNDERSTANDING

In the preface to the 2001 edition of her book *The Women in the Body*, Emily Martin contrasts two ways of understanding menstruation. In the presiding account, the body is a mechanical system, and normal menstruation involves regular periodic cycles:

> Estrogen, progesterone and other hormones are produced...with machine-like regularity; menstruation occurs...with the periodicity of a metronome. Disease produces irregularity; and shifts between stages of menstruation (puberty and early menopause) produce irregularity. Regularity is normal, good and valued; irregularity is abnormal and negatively valued.[15]

Now suppose we take a tip from current thinking about the heart. According to Martin, cardiologists increasingly understand the heart not as a mechanical pump but as a self-organizing system with chaotic dynamics that become regular only near death. Chaotic systems have advantages: They are flexible, adaptable, and can operate within a range of different situations. Indeed, Martin quotes research according to which "the heart and other physiological systems may behave most erratically when they are young and healthy."[16] Suppose we were to transfer this understanding of health to menstruation. Martin writes:

> We could describe irregularity as an adaptive response to a changing internal and external environment. The young woman whose menstrual cycle is affected by exercise, by stress, or by puberty could then think what a good job her endocrine system is doing flexibly adjusting to her life, rather than worrying about a pathological "irregularity." Epidemiological studies that have shown greater menstrual irregularity in women who work at night...and women who are vegetarians...could be taken to reveal the responsiveness of these women's physiological systems to their particular environment, rather than a pathological deviation from a putative norm of machine-like periodicity. The older women whose menstrual cycle is affected by approaching menopause...could do the same. Here it would be particularly gratifying to see irregularity as a sign of vigor and health instead of impending disease and death.[17]

For our purposes, this contrast between understanding irregularity as a problem and understanding it as a sign of health illustrates the importance of how we understand. If irregularity is a medical problem, it follows that we ought to fix it; if, however, it is a sign of health, it follows that we should not. But how ought we to understand it? What are the standards or marks of accurate, or at least defensible, understandings versus indefensible ones? In what follows, I return to Gadamer's hermeneutics to explore his answer to this question. Then, I apply it to our understanding of sex and gender,

In appealing to Gadamer, Alcoff stresses the horizons from which we understand. Yet, our horizons do not exhaust the process of understanding. Rather, in Gadamer's view, we must also attend to the way our initial, horizonal orientation toward that which we are trying to understand works out in our actual understanding. Gadamer concentrates on the understanding of textual meaning. We begin to read a text from a particular horizon that affords us a particular orientation to it. We might expect, for example, that given our twenty-first-century horizon, we will find in Jane Austen's *Pride and Prejudice* an old-fashioned and even moldy picture of the charms of love and marriage, so we prepare ourselves for boredom. Yet, as we read its very first sentence, we realize we are in for something quite different; we are in for humor and for satire. This realization becomes a new horizon for trying to understand the rest of the novel. Coming to understand the text is a process of projecting an account of its meaning, revising that projection in line with our understanding of new parts of the text, integrating our understanding of previous parts of the text in line with the new projection, and repeating this process until we have finished the book and integrated all its parts into a coherent whole. The process of understanding is thus a circular one: We read the whole in terms of the parts, and the parts in terms of the whole, in an attempt to understand the meaning of the text as an internally consistent unity.

Here, we might ask why we should assume that a text—or, indeed, whatever we are trying to understand—really *is* an internally consistent unity of meaning. After all, deconstructive approaches to texts start with the opposite assumption: Texts inevitably fail in their attempts to form coherent wholes, and the best textual readings look not for the text's unity but rather for its fissures, for points in the text where what is not said undermines what is said, or where what is said is more than what the text admits to saying.[18] Other approaches to texts stop short of declaring that all texts fail as unities but nonetheless admit to some caution about beginning with an assumption in favor of their unity. Authors certainly write texts over a period of months or years; why assume they do not change their minds, whether subtly or not? Why assume they mean to write an internally consistent text? Why, should hermeneuticists typically insist upon coherence?

For Gadamer, assuming that a text coheres as a unity of meaning is a condition of understanding it at all.[19] We can reconstruct his reasoning as follows: Any understanding we have of meaning is a horizonal one, for horizons are our modes of access to the world. While we can broaden, and even change, our horizons, we cannot exchange them for no horizon at all. Yet, if not, how can we judge the accuracy of what our horizons allow us to see? How can we determine whether a particular reading is at all faithful to the meaning of a text—or, to enlarge the scope of hermeneutic beyond texts as Alcoff does, to situations, events, actions, and the like? Alcoff ties the answer to such questions to our projects; the worth of a particular horizon and what it allows us to see depends upon the projects we possess. This answer, however, is not completely satisfactory, because it neglects the possibility that we may want to—or, in fact, ought to—reflect on our projects. Moreover, it prevents us from considering whether or not our projects allow us an adequate understanding of a text or situation. If, for example, our project is that of stabilizing the landed gentry, we may institutionalize the queen's understanding of the castle without considering what it excludes and whether it makes sense.

The hermeneutic circle is Gadamer's answer to arbitrary understandings. Given that we cannot have a non-horizonal understanding of meaning, we can determine the adequacy or faithfulness of the understanding a particular horizon allows only if we employ this understanding as a foil for testing itself, using its parts to confirm our understanding of the whole and the whole to confirm our understanding of its parts. Unless we assume that the text forms a coherent whole, the failure of any one part of our understanding to fit with another can be no cause for questioning our understanding as a whole, or vice versa. Conversely, assuming the coherence of the text or a text-analogue, such as an event, situation, or practice, gives us a basis for revising our understandings of its parts if they fail to fit together and our understanding of the whole if that understanding does not allow us to make sense out of the parts. By presuming that the text is internally consistent, we allow our horizonal understanding of meaning to try to justify itself.

Although Gadamer follows the hermeneutic tradition as a whole in conceiving of this circle as a means of testing and revising understandings, he differs from some of his predecessors in maintaining the multiplicity of possible readings of part and whole. Alcoff notes that within a given time and place, those who are differently socially positioned, such as queen and servant, can have different horizons on meaning. Gadamer more often stresses historical differences. Thus, Mary Favret explains that because of England's recent experience with industrialization, late Victorian English readers understood Austen's work in terms of "a pious, domestic femininity at ease in a sanitized, pre-industrial world."[20] Compare this understanding with contemporary readings that find in Austen's work homoerotic love between sisters (*Sense and Sensibility* in Eve Sedgwick's reading[21]) and an "outrageous unconventionality" that undermines dominant contemporaneous values (*Pride and Prejudice* in Claudia L. Johnson's reading[22]). Such newer readings of Austen issue from horizons landscaped by queer theory and feminism, respectively, and they reflect situated modes of access quite different than those of the Victorians. In general, given their different experiences, different historical eras will understand the same text differently. Indeed, Gadamer maintains that "[e]very age has to understand a transmitted text in its own way."[23] History continues: New events happen; cultures arise, fall, and interact; new texts are written; and these events, cultures, and texts cast the older ones in a new light. What was the Great War of 1914 to 1917 becomes World War I. What may have been daily life for Austen's first readers becomes a dear and fading memory for Victorians. And what is a dear and fading memory for the Victorians becomes a caldron of incestuous desires and subversive acts for contemporary readers.

At the same time, this multiplicity of successful interpretations does not mean all, or even any, understanding of a text, event, culture, or the like is plausible. Whereas a form of what Alcoff calls a dysfunctional relativism may insist that any understanding of meaning is as good as any other, a hermeneutic position holds that only some are as good as others—and that some are not. But what distinguishes the latter? If the integrity of whole and part provides a criterion for a successful understanding, the lack of integration provides a criterion for an unsuccessful one. It may be that what we are trying to understand in fact fails to compose a unity; it may be poorly thought out, fragmentary, or the like. It may also be that we simply have a bad vantage point for seeing what the text or text-analogue is, so we cannot complete the circle of whole and part. Early anthropological understandings of *berdaches* can be evaluated in these terms. Relying uncritically on their own cultural horizon, anthropologists understood *berdaches* as homosexuals, and they failed to check this understanding against other aspects of the native cultures under study. In effect, early anthropologists failed to check whether an interpretation of *berdaches* as homosexuals could be integrated within the native cultures' institutions and practices as a whole—institutions and practices that distinguished *berdaches* from homosexuals, sissies, and a series of other identities. Early anthropologists also thereby missed an opportunity to reflect on their own conceptions of gender. Where we fail in our attempts to unify part and whole, it may sometimes be necessary to expand, or even change, our horizons in order to understand in a way that these early anthropologists did not. Certainly one virtue of a conscientious hermeneutic approach is its ever-present awareness that such a change may be necessary. In any case, we can distinguish between better and worse understandings in terms of their relative success in integrating part and whole.

How does this extended account of Gadamer's hermeneutics help us in reflecting on sex and gender? We try to understand many things, and among them are texts, situations, actions, and who we are. And whatever else they are, sex and gender are ways for us to understand who we and others are. It follows, then, that if we can understand others and ourselves as sexes and/or genders, these understandings should mirror the conditions for a successful understanding of texts. In other words, they should be capable of unifying part and whole. The question, then, is if—and, if so, when—they can.

UNDERSTANDING SEX AND GENDER

When we can claim to understand a text, we can display an understanding of its parts in terms of its whole and an understanding of its whole in terms of its parts. Thus, if the horizon we possess on Austen's *Mansfield Park* allows us to understand it as a plea for stability, we can understand the character of Fanny Price as a conservative figure among a group of shallow peers with facile notions of change. Of course, we may understand the novel from a different horizon, such as the horizon of an outsider, and therefore stress the extent to which Fanny's character stems from both her exclusion from the Bertram family and her awareness of the illicit nature of her love for Edmund.[24] If we take this perspective on Fanny, we understand the text itself differently as well—not as a conservative novel perhaps but as a subversive one in which the outsider and illicit lover triumphs. How we understand the novel determines who we understand Fanny Price to be, just as how we understand Fanny Price determines what we take the novel to be. We can make a similar point about non-textual understanding by returning to ways of understanding the heart. For here what provokes researchers to rethink this organ is a discovery or series of discoveries that cannot be integrated with previous accounts of what it is. If our current understanding of irregularity conceives of it as a sign of health rather than of disease, then we must also change the way we understand what the heart is: We can no longer see it as a pump; rather, we must now understand it as a chaotic system.

What about our understanding of who we are? Like understandings of texts, understandings of identities move in a circle of wholes and parts in which the wholes of which we are parts are the "texts," as it were, of our on-going lives. If our understanding of Fanny Price depends upon our understanding of *Mansfield Park*, and if our understanding of hearts depends upon our understanding of chaotic systems, then our understanding of who we are depends upon our understanding of the contexts in which we live and act. Yet, we live and act in many contexts. If Fanny

Price lives only in *Mansfield Park*, we live in many narratives: the story of our families, the arc of our careers, the plot or plots of our country or historical era. We are also parts of our friends and acquaintances' stories, and to the extent that we interact with strangers, we are part of their stories as well. But if we are parts of many stories, and if these stories are the contexts, the wholes, that determine our meanings as parts, it follows that we have many meanings—or in other words, many identities. There are, it turns out, many different ways of saying who we are, and these depend on the many different contexts or wholes of which we find ourselves a part. Within families, we can be understood as parents, children, brothers, and sisters. Within history as a whole, we might be better understood as members of a postindustrial society. Within our working lives, we can be understood as professionals, white-collar workers, unemployed, and so on. In every case, how we can be intelligibly or coherently understood depends upon the text or context within which the question of who we are arises and into which our identity must be integrated, just as our understanding of the text or context depends, in part, upon our understanding of who we are.

At least three consequences follow. First, there are as many plausible ways of understanding who we and others are as there are contexts in which we and others move, act, and interact. We are sisters, perhaps, in a family, and we are Democrats, perhaps, in the voting booth. Second, there are many different ways of understanding those contexts and therefore who we are in them. Hence, within the meaning that family has in a particular culture, we may, or may not, be understandable as sisters; at the same time, what families are in a particular culture will depend upon who in that culture counts as sisters. Third, within the different contexts in which we move, act, and interact—contexts that can be understood in different ways—we can also be understood in different ways. Thus, we can understand Fanny as a conservative or a subversive within the context of *Mansfield Park*, which itself is thereby understood as a conservative or a subversive novel. Likewise, we may be seen as good sisters or bad ones with reference to a family, which is itself thereby intelligible as a certain kind of family.

What are the consequences of this analysis for our understanding of others and ourselves as men and women and as males and females? First, as ways of understanding who we are, they are bound within specific stories and wholes. They are not, in other words, acontextual and always plausible ways of understanding our identities but rather ways that are more or less intelligible depending upon the interpretive context in which they appear. Second, there will be different ways of understanding those contexts and therefore who counts as males and females or as men and women within them. Within the meaning a context or story has in a particular culture, we may, or may not, be understandable as women or as females. Third, our understandings of men and women and of males and females will depend upon the understanding of the contexts in which we can successfully see them as parts. I want to look at each of these consequences more carefully, starting with their implications for males and females.

What are the wholes for which sexed identities as males and females are parts? One such whole would seem to be sexual reproduction. Just as Fanny Price is Fanny Price within the context of *Mansfield Park*, females and males are females and males within the story of sexual reproduction. There will be different ways that different interpreters can understand sexual reproduction, however. Adrienne Rich and Judith Butler understand it as compulsory heterosexuality, for instance, and therefore understand as its parts not so much males and females as heterosexuals and even heteronormative beings. Moreover, if we can be understood as males and females within the context of sexual reproduction, we can understand males and females in different ways. They may be those who contribute sperm and eggs, respectively, to the proceedings or those who engage in the sort of sex that can conceivably issue in children. Finally, in either case, if sexual reproduction, however understood, is the only whole or context into which we can coherently integrate identities as males and females, then sex will not be a coherent way to understand who we are outside of it. After all, however we understand Fanny Price, we cannot understand her at all outside of the context of the novel.

Are there other contexts or stories, then, into which we can coherently integrate identities as males and females? Can we write a sequel to *Mansfield Park*, as it were, in order to find an expanded place for Fanny? Do not all biologically constituted contexts provide wholes within which we can be understood as males or females? Londa Schiebinger tells us that it has only been since the eighteenth century that every part of our bodies—except perhaps our eyes—has been understood to be male or female. Moreover, as she points out, the finding stemmed from a political agenda—namely, trying to ensure that exclusions of women from all public spheres had a biological basis.[25] It remains unclear, however, whether understanding the heart, for example, as a female heart has helped or hindered medical diagnoses. I think is it far more plausible to say that in contexts of non-reproductive biology, males and females are square pegs in a round hole. Take medical contexts in general. Is it clear that understanding patients as males or females has any justification? We delay in noticing that certain individuals have heart disease because we understand them as females and think that females rarely have heart disease; we delay in noticing that other individuals have breast cancer because we understand them as males and think that males rarely have breast cancer. In general, a better understanding of the identities that form intelligible or coherent parts of medical contexts would seem to be identities as patients. We do not cater medical treatments to people understood as Red Sox fans or Yankee fans, Iowans or Californians. Does it make any more sense to cater them to people understood as males or females? Should we not understand them rather as ill people or healthy ones?

In this connection, we might return to the case of Thomas Beatie. Recall that Beatie retained his original internal organs after transitioning to living as man and, because he and his wife wanted a baby, intentionally became pregnant. One might think that most of the pertinent medical questions would center on his identity as a pregnant person and be concerned with his health and the health of the fetus. Instead, most questions centered on his identity as a male or a female. Could he legitimately claim to be male, or was he self-deluded in thinking he was? Was he, as he claimed, his own surrogate, or was he just a female pretending to be a male?

In one interpretation, these questions are not completely odd. Sexual reproduction is the context within which such questioners situate and try to understand who Beatie is. Females can be understood to form integral parts of this context, and given Beatie's functions within it, understanding him as a female is not a bad understanding. Yet, even in this case, surely we cannot understand him as a female outside of the context of sexual reproduction. At most, we can understand and designate him as a female only for the amount of time during which he consents to being pregnant. In a second interpretation, the context for understanding Beatie is that of pregnancy, the parts of which are pregnant people and non-pregnant people. Here, the issue of their sex simply does not arise. This way of integrating part and whole has a certain advantage over the first, I think. It allows us to focus on the prenatal care that actual pregnant people need, and it allow us to forego the sorts of unanswerable questions those around Beatie raised, such as whether Beatie have a right to say he was. Ultimately, we can take up either horizon: that of sexual reproduction or that of pregnancy. It bears repeating, however, that even in the first case, any understanding of Thomas Beatie as a female has a limited scope and that the second understanding might be better for the project of appropriate medical care.

We can raise similar reservations about the possibly untoward breadth of our understandings of gender identities. Insofar as they must conform to the conditions of understanding, their intelligibility is tied to specific contexts, which themselves are understood in specific ways, and within those contexts, gender identities can be understood in different ways. To begin with, then, into which context or contexts can we coherently integrate identities as women or as men? Of which wholes are they parts? Premodern and early modern Europe contained men and women as part of a metaphysical whole. At one point, both democracy and education were also understood in gender terms, excluding women. Yet, although they continue to be understood in this way in some countries, they do so to the condemnation of the rest of the world. One context, however, in which individuals in many parts of the world and in much of the United States continue to be adamantly understood as men and women is marriage. According to the laws of many U.S. states and the federal Defense of Marriage Act,[26] we understand the individuals who compose the parties to marriage as men and women, and we are to understand marriage as the union between one man and one woman.

Yet, despite these laws, it is not clear that marriage is best understood in this way, or that it provides a plausible context for identities as men and women.[27] What, we might ask, is marriage? How should we understand it? William M. Hohengarten echoes the approach we have taken here by trying to understand what he describes as the law on domestic relations in the context of the constitutional law of privacy.[28] What function, he asks, does civil or legal marriage serve? His answer is that it offers "a legal medium through which two adults can make a mutual commitment to stay together."[29] Two adults can, of course, commit to one another to stay together without getting married, but what distinguishes marriage from such a commitment is its legal enforceability. I can walk away from a committed relationship, but if I want to end my marriage, I have to get divorced. Moreover, even given no-fault divorce laws that allow the end of a marriage if either partner takes steps to end it, that partner must still take those steps. The costs of divorcing are still higher than the costs of simply walking away.

Given this understanding of marriage, it is unclear why anyone would choose it. It costs time and money to dissolve a marriage, so what is to be gained by it? There are, of course, a host of economic and status benefits to marriage: Federal law contains 1,049 of them.[30] Nevertheless, committed couples could try to reproduce at least some of these through individual contracts. They could adopt one another's children in order to enjoy full rights as their parents; they could prepare wills and health care proxies to secure each other's futures; in some states, they could even claim health insurance for one another. So why get married? Hohengarten suggests that what marriage gives a couple is the right to present themselves to the world as a unit, and because they are unit, their relationship is guaranteed the same privacy that an individual is. His example here is the New York case of *Brashi v. Stahl Associates*. The issue in this case was whether the surviving partner of a same-sex relationship should count as family and therefore have the right to stay in the rent-controlled apartment the couple had shared. The court said yes, but it devised a rather rigorous test for deciding whether a given relationship could pass muster:

> The determination as to whether an individual is entitled to non-eviction protection should be based upon an objective examination of the relationship of the parties. In making this assessment, the lower courts of this state have looked to a number of factors, including the exclusivity and longevity of the relationship, the level of emotional and financial commitment, the manner in which the parties have conducted their everyday lives and held themselves out to society, and the reliance placed upon one another for daily family services. These factors are most helpful, although it should be emphasized that the presence of absence of one of more of them is not dispositive since it is the totality of the relationship as evidenced by the dedication, caring and self-sacrifice of the parties which should in the final analysis, control.[31]

Hohengarten observes, "It is little wonder that other courts in other circumstances have found this inquiry to be beyond their institutional competence."[32] Yet, the more important point for our purposes is that had the couple been able to marry, the surviving partner would have been able to stay in the apartment regardless of the nature of their relationship. Because marriage creates a legally binding unit, those who are married have rights to conduct their relationship in any way they want, without risking their status as a married couple or providing the state with a reason to examine their daily lives. To this extent, civil marriage provides a no-questions-asked legitimacy. One need not prove the intimacy of one's relationship to have access to a spouse who is in the hospital; one need not carry around documents showing that one has legal rights to the children of the marriage; one need not demonstrate commitment to one's spouse in order to inherit his or her property.

Given this understanding of marriage, who has the right to marry? Put in hermeneutic terms, how should we understand those who can get married? The weight of U.S. Supreme Court decisions on marriage seems to lean in a direction opposed to that codified in the Defense of Marriage Act. In 1948, the California Supreme Court became the first state court to rescind anti-miscegenation statutes outlawing civil marriages between whites and non-whites. In finding the anti-miscegenation law and its various amendments to violate the state constitution, the court declared that the right to marry was the right "to join in marriage with the person of one's choice."[33] The U.S. Supreme Court followed suit in 1967, invalidating all restrictions on the right to marry based on racial classifications.[34] In subsequent decisions, the Supreme Court invalidated laws prohibiting marriage for prison inmates[35] and for non-custodial parents who were too poor to support their children from previous relationships.[36] The tendency of these cases is to peel a series of identities off of the institution of marriage in order to clarify which identities can be coherently understood to be parts of it. Civil marriage, the Supreme Court says, does not include whites or non-whites, free people or prison inmates or custodial or non-custodial parents. Rather, the implication of the Court's decisions is that as a right to marry the person of one's choice, the institution is composed of only choosers and those who consent to be chosen. As such, it also fails to include either men and women or males and females.

Advocates for conceiving of marriage as an institution limited to identities as men and women sometimes appeal to the needs of parenting. Indeed, they maintain that the very point of civil marriage as an institution is to protect and nurture children. Children, they argue, do best in two-parent families consisting of a man and a woman, because men and women differ from one another and their different virtues benefit their children.[37] As the New York court rejecting marriage between same-sex partners put the point, "Intuition and experience suggest that a child benefits from having before his or her eyes, every day, living models of what both a man and a woman are like."[38] Yet, here we have to ask, what *are* a man and a woman like? The empirical studies we looked at in Chapter One had a difficult time answering this question. French theory and concerns with intersectionality only complicate the issue. Even George Dent, a fan of the man-woman nuclear household, admits, "No law forbids an effeminate man to marry a masculine woman."[39] Nor is there any law prohibiting an effeminate man from marrying an effeminate woman, or a masculine man from marrying a masculine woman. So where in these marriages are the complementary qualities that are meant to make a difference when raising children? Moreover, how can parenting serve as a context for understanding others or ourselves as men and women? Are we not better understood as good parents or bad ones?

Consider some of the contradictions to which courts are forced in allowing gender and, in addition, sex into marriage. Sterling Simmons was born Bessie Lewis in 1959, but in 1991, he obtained a total abdominal hysterectomy and a bilateral salpingo-oophorectomy to remove his uterus, fallopian tubes, and ovaries. In 1994, his doctor submitted an affidavit certifying that Simmons had received certain operations, and Simmons received a new birth certificate designating his sex as male. He subsequently married a woman, and when his wife gave birth to a child through artificial insemination, he was listed as the father on the infant's birth certificate. Yet, when the couple then tried to divorce, an Illinois court claimed that their marriage had never been valid in the first place.[40] Moreover, the court awarded sole custody of the child to the former (non) wife, determining that Simmons lacked both parental rights and the standing to seek custody. Simmons appealed the result, but in 1998, the appeals court affirmed the trial court's opinion: The marriage was invalid, and Simmons had no parental rights. In the reasoning of the appeals court, Simmons was a woman because, although he had had various operations to remove internal organs, he had not completed work on his breasts or undergone the scrotoplasty, urethroplasty, and phalloplasty that would have created a penis.[41] Because lesbian couples do not have the right to marry in Illinois, the marriage never existed, and without marriage, Simmons' rights as a parent never existed either.

Take another case, however. A male-to-female transsexual named Christie Littleton sued her late husband's physician for wrongful death because of the medical treatment he had received.[42] In 2000, the Fourth Circuit Court of Appeals of Texas ruled against her suit not on the basis of the facts of the case but on her lack of standing as the surviving spouse to bring the suit in the first place. Here, the court relied on both the federal Defense of Marriage Act and on Texas laws outlawing marriages between same-sex partners. Of course, Christie Littleton did not consider herself a man or a homosexual. Nevertheless, for the court, the question was whether Christie was legally a woman. The court conceded, "Her self-identity, from childhood, has been as a woman," and "[s]ince her various operations, she does not have the outward physical characteristics of a man."[43] The court also distinguished between transvestites, whom it defined as men who gain "some sexual satisfaction from wearing women's clothes," and Littleton, who "does not consider herself a man wearing women's clothes; she considers herself a woman wearing women's clothes."[44] The court even acknowledged the possibility of "using the surgical removal of the male genitalia as the test" for womanhood and agreed with Littleton's lawyer that "amputation is a pretty important step."[45] Nevertheless, in the end, the court came to a conclusion about sex based on chromosomal facts. "Biologically," it said, a "post-operative female transsexual is still a male."[46]

If we look at the legal opinion about Sterling Simmons' sex and gender, we find that the absence of a penis was sufficient, despite his role as a husband and father, to make him female and a woman. If we look at the legal opinion on Christie Littleton's sex and gender, however, neither the absence of a penis nor her role as a wife was sufficient to make her a woman. In Texas, the only way to change one's sex, at least for the purposes of civil marriage, is to change one's chromosomes—not yet a medical possibility. And the only way to be a woman is to have the sex of a female. Noting differences among various states and between the states and the federal government, one of Littleton's lawyer's drew the consequences for her:

> Mrs. Littleton, while in San Antonio, Tex., is a male and has a void marriage; as she travels to Houston, Tex., and enters federal property, she is female and a widow; upon traveling to Kentucky, she is female and a widow; but, upon entering Ohio, she is once again male and prohibited from marriage; entering Connecticut, she is again female and may marry; if her travel takes her north to Vermont, she is male and may marry a female; if instead she travels south to New Jersey, she may marry a male.[47]

We might ask the courts to formulate a uniform code that tells us who counts as males and females and as men and women. But we might also ask two other questions: first, whether marriage really involves these identities at all and, second, whether we can be understood in terms of these identities in most of the contexts in which we spend our lives. For if it is difficult to conceive of a context for identities as males and females other than sexual reproduction, it is difficult to conceive of any modern contexts of which gender is a part. To be sure, failing to conceive of such contexts does not mean that there are none. At the same time, recognizing that sex and gender identities are specific to particular contexts offers a way of accounting for contradictions such as those we have found in legal understandings. These contradictions issue from the attempt to understand sex and gender identities in contexts where those identities simply make no sense. In general, to assume that we are always male or female and men or women is to find Fanny Price in every book we read.

Alcoff employs hermeneutics to illuminate the way the lived experience of having breasts, menstruating, and being capable of bearing children secures an interpretive horizon very different from a horizon not founded on these possessions and capacities. In contrast, I have employed hermeneutics to explore the conditions of understanding. For if, as Martin tells us, we can understand menstruation differently, as either a regular or a chaotic system, then surely we can understand our lived experience of it differently as well. The same would seem to hold for possessing breasts, which have not only different sizes but also different meanings for different people, and for being able to bear children. Of course, it may be that sex and gender do provide horizons that differ in crucial ways for men and women. But before we say that they do, we need to make sure that we understand what sex and gender are and within which contexts they are intelligible identities to understand us to possess.

CHAPTER SIX

Conclusion

The terms *sex* and *gender* possess a deceptive clarity. Perhaps the most basic question the terms raise is whether sex and gender are really distinct. In Chapter One we considered research claiming that so-called gender is simply an outgrowth of so-called sex. Thus, while some feminist scholars denied that women's position in history and society could be laid at the feet of their biology—or in other words, their sex—others insisted that because of hormones, brain structure, and other biological features, at least parts of it most certainly could.

Arguments against this view take defensive and offensive forms. Some scholars carefully examine the arguments that are meant to show that masculine and feminine genders directly map onto male and female sexes.[1] In large part, these scholars claim, arguments that purport to show the way in which sex causes gender either fail or beg the question. Others take the offensive and question the terms of the debate. In their view, those who claim that sex causes gender and those who claim that it does not both presume that the distinction between sex and gender maps easily onto other dichotomies: between nature and nurture and between the physical body and historical culture. Yet, these critics say, this presumption is surely debatable. First, we need to ask whether the sex/body/nature side of the dichotomy is really outside of history and non-cultural. Bodies are certainly changed by history—by better nutrition, for example—as well as by culture: Recall the image of a person outside in the sun and, although therefore able to absorb vitamin D, covered head to toe in a burka. Historical changes and cultural variations also affect those parts of bodies credited with their sex. Young girls now hit puberty earlier than they once did, and environmental changes are said to be the cause of decreases in sperm count and of increases in testicular cancer.[2] Second, some theorists argue that the idea that certain parts of the body constitute its sex already presupposes gender. A perspective from which breasts and genitalia link up with one another as indices of a person's sex is a perspective conditioned by the human interest in reproduction. Universal as this interest may be, many theorists insist that it signals the extent to which human interests conceptually carve nature to fit those interests—the extent, then, to which culture is responsible for nature and gender for sex.[3]

If sex dissolves into gender, however, questions about gender abound. In the first place, if gender is either autonomous of sex or swallows it whole, then it need not be tethered to any particular sort of body. In Chapter Two, we surveyed some of the different possible relations between gender and bodies, including *berdaches* and sworn virgins. In separating gender as a non-hierarchical category from men and women as hierarchical ones, Sally Haslanger adds more genders, proposing to replace those of men and women with different ones, such as pregnant persons and infertile ones. For her part, Kate Bornstein aims to replace them with such identities as tops and bottoms. Other scholars think gender itself is problematic. Some maintain that it is nothing more than a relation between linguistic terms: Women are not men, but if men are not women, where does our definition touch ground? Some argue gender is entwined with, at a minimum, race and class, but doubtlessly also with sexuality, age, postcoloniality, ability, and in fact, such an ever-increasing number of factors that it is not clear what it actually is. There are those who therefore try to reconceptualize it in such a way that it can incorporate difference while still serving as a useful category for analyses of injustice and inequality. And there are also those who try to analyze injustice and inequality without gender at all, or with a conception of gender that they concede remains split, subdivided, and contestable.

In Chapter Five, I suggested that both sex and gender are simply ways of understanding who we and others are and, as such, that they must conform to the conditions of understanding. These conditions involve the hermeneutic circle of whole and part: We understand meanings within contexts in which our understandings of meaning and context reciprocally constitute each other. I used the example of textual understanding to make this point: We understand the parts of a text in terms of its whole and the whole in terms of its parts. Likewise, when we take certain individuals to be men or women, males or females, we understand them within specific stories and contexts, which themselves are understood in certain ways. To understand someone as a male or a female is to situate that person conceptually within the context of sexual reproduction; to understand someone as a man or woman is to situate that person conceptually within some other context.

To be sure, I am not clear what the contexts for understandings in terms of gender are. Nevertheless, like those for sex, they are limited however we specify them. To understand others or ourselves as males and females, or as men and women, in all contexts violates the part-whole conditions of understanding. We can understand Fanny Price as Fanny Price only as long as she remains part of the story of *Mansfield Park*. We can understand men and women as men and women, or understand males and females as males and females, only in similarly circumscribed ways. As ways of understanding who we and others are, sex and gender have a limited purview. Outside of it, we shall have to understand others and ourselves differently: as patients, baseball fans, and professors, perhaps. And perhaps this conclusion is the solution to the questions and debates we have surveyed in this book. Contained in their niches, as ways of understanding others and ourselves, sex and gender take their place beside other ways of understanding who we are. For who we are depends upon who is asking and with regard to what.

Notes

INTRODUCTION

1. Toril Moi, *What Is a Woman? And Other Essays* (Oxford: Oxford University Press, 1999), p. 15.

CHAPTER ONE

1. Gayle Rubin, "The Traffic in Women: Notes on the 'Political Economy of Sex' (1975)" in *The Second Wave: A Reader in Feminist Theory*, ed. Linda Nicholson (New York: Routledge, 1997) p. 32.
2. Simone de Beauvoir, *The Second Sex* (1949), trans. and ed. H. M. Parshley (New York: Knopf, Everyman's Library, 1993).
3. John Money and Anke Ehrhardt, *Man and Woman, Boy and Girl: The Differentiation and Dimorphism of Gender Identity from Conception to Maturity* (Baltimore: John Hopkins University Press, 1972). Moi claims that although Money first coined the distinction, it was Robert J. Stoller's formulation of the distinction that "fired feminists' imagination." (*What Is a Woman*, p. 22; note 29.) Stoller cites Money's essay "An Examination of Some Basic Sexual Concepts: The Evidence of Human Hermaphrodism" in *Bulletin of the Johns Hopkins Hospital*, Vol. 97, No. 1 (1955), pp. 301–19.
4. See *What is a Woman*.
5. *The Second Sex*, p. 281.
6. Ibid., p. xlv.
7. Ibid., p. 30.
8. All quotations on pregnancy and nursing are from *The Second Sex*, p. 31.
9. Ibid., p. 28.
10. Ibid., p. 34.
11. Ibid., p. 33.
12. Ibid., p. 67.

13. Ibid., p. 68.

14. Ibid., p. 67.

15. Ibid., p. 68.

16. Ibid., p. 69.

17. Ibid., p. lix.

18. Ibid., p. 474.

19. Ibid., p. 66.

20. Ibid., p. 68.

21. K. Hawkes, J. F. O'Connell, and N. G. Blurton Jones, "Hadza Women's Time Allocation, Offspring Provisioning and the Evolution of Long Postmenopausal Life Spans" in *Current Anthropology*, Vol. 38, No. 4 (1997), p. 557.

22. Sarah Blaffer Hrdy, *Mother Nature: Maternal Instincts and How They Shape the Human Species* (New York: Ballantine Books, 1999), p. 285.

23. Ibid., p. 287.

24. *The Second Sex*, p. 476–7.

25. Ibid., pp. 542 and 550, respectively.

26. Ibid., p. 36.

27. For analyses of Beauvoir's account of the body and possible tensions in her comparison of the causal roles of biology with those of history or culture, see Karen Vintges, "*The Second Sex* and Philosophy" and Julie K. Ward, "Beauvoir's Two Senses of 'Body' in *The Second Sex*" in *Feminist Interpretations of Simone de Beauvoir*, ed. Margaret A. Simons (New York: Routledge, 1995). Also see Penelope Deutscher, *Yielding Gender: Feminism, Deconstruction and the History of Philosophy* (New York: Routledge, 1997), Chapter 7.

28. *The Second Sex*, p. 285.

29. Ibid., p. 292.

30. Ibid., p. 293.

31. Ibid., p. 294–5.

32. Ibid., p. 303.

33. Ibid., pp. xlv-xlvi.

34. Ibid., p. xlviii.

35. We return to this issue in Chapter 4, where we again take up Beauvoir's position on race, class, and gender. Here, we are concerned only to establish the distinction between sex and gender that Second Wave Feminism found useful.

36. *The Second Sex*, p. l.

37. See Ruth Hubbard, "Gender and Genitals: Constructs of Sex and Gender" in *Social Text*, Nos. 46/47, (Spring-Summer1996), pp. 157–165, 157.

38. *Man and Woman, Boy and Girl*, p. 14.

39. Ibid., p. 13.

40. Ibid, p. 4.
41. Ibid., p. 4.
42. Ibid.
43. Ibid., p. 13.
44. Ibid., p. 152.
45. I also discuss this case in Chapter One of *After Identity: Rethinking Race, Sex and Gender* (Cambridge: Cambridge University Press, 2007). Both children eventually committed suicide.
46. John Colapinto, *As Nature Made Him: The Boy Who Was Raised as a Girl* (New York: Perennial, 2001), p. 81.
47. See *Man and Woman, Boy and Girl*, pp. 118–123.
48. Judith Butler, "Sex and Gender in Simone de Beauvoir's *Second Sex*" in *Yale French Studies*, No. 72 (1986), p. 35.
49. *As Nature Made Him*, p. 61.
50. Ibid., p. 57.
51. Cited in Milton Diamond, "Sexual Identity, Monozygotic Twins Reared in Discordant Sex Roles and a BBC Follow up," *Archives of Sexual Behavior*, Vol. 11, No. 2 (1982). p. 183.
52. See Milton Diamond and Keith Sigmundson, "Sex Reassignment at Birth: Long-Term Review and Clinical Implications" in *Archives of Pediatric and Adolescent Medicine*, Vol. 151, No. 3, (1997), pp. 298–304.
53. J. Imperato-McGinley, R. E. Peterson, T. Gautier, and E. Sturla, "Androgens and the evolution of male-gender identity among male pseudohermaphrodites with 5-alpha reductase deficiency" in *New England Journal of Medicine*, Vol. 300, No. 22 (1979), pp. 1233–7.
54. Cited from Gilbert Herdt, "Mistaken Sex: Culture, Biology and the Third Sex in New Guinea" in *Third Sex/Third Gender: Beyond Sexual Dimorphism in Culture and History*, ed. Gilbert Herdt (New York: Zone Books, 1994) p.426.
55. "William G. Reiner. and John P. Gearhard, "Discordant Sexual Identity in Some Genetic Males with Cloacal Exstrophy Assigned to Female Sex at Birth" in *The New England Journal of Medicine*, Vol. 350, No. 4 (2004), p. 338.
56. Ibid, p. 336.
57. Ibid.,
58. *As Nature Made Him*, pp. 86–7.
59. See "Mistaken Sex," pp. 427–8.
60. See Anne Fausto-Sterling, *Myths of Gender: Biological Theories about Women and Men*, rev. ed. (New York: Basic Books, 1992), p. 87.
61. Heino F. L. Meyer-Bahlburg, "Gender identity outcome in female-raised 46,XY persons with penile agenesis, cloacal exstrophy of the bladder, or penile ablation" in *Archives of Sexual Behavior* (2005) pp. 423–438.

62. Ibid., p. 432.
63. Ibid.
64. Ibid.
65. Ibid.
66. Ibid., p. 433.
67. Ibid.
68. Ibid.
69. Ibid.
70. Ibid.
71. "Discordant Sexual Identity in Some Genetic Males with Cloacal Exstrophy," p. 338.
72. Ibid.
73. Robert Wright, *The Moral Animal: Why We Are the Way We Are* (New York: Random House Vintage Books, 1995) p. 31
74. See Bobbi S. Low, *Why Sex Matters: A Darwinian Look at Human Behavior* (Princeton, NJ: Princeton University Press, 2000), p. 43.
75. *The Moral Animal*, p. 51.
76. Ibid.
77. Ibid., p. 46.
78. Mary Soares Masters and Barbara Sanders, "Is the gender difference in mental rotation disappearing?" in *Journal of Behavior Genetics*, Vol. 23, No. 4 (1993), pp. 337–41.
79. Neil V. Watson and Doreen Kimura, "Nontrivial sex differences in throwing and intercepting: Relation to psychometrically-defined spatial functions" in *Personality and Individual Differences*, Vol. 12, No. 5 (1991), pp. 375–85.
80. Scott Moffat, Elizabeth Hampson, and Maria Hatzipantelis, "Navigation in a 'Virtual' Maze: Sex Differences and Correlation with Psychometric Measures of Spatial Ability in Humans" in *Evolution and Human Behavior*, Vol. 19, No. 2 (1998), pp. 73–87.
81. Deborah Blum, *Sex on the Brain: The Biological Differences between Men and Women* (New York: Penguin Books, 1997), p. 58.
82. Simon Baron-Cohen, Rebecca C. Knickmeyer, and Matthew K. Belmonte, "Sex Differences in the Brain: Implications for Explaining Autism" in *Science*, Vol. 310, No. 5749 (2005), pp. 819–23.
83. Ibid.
84. Anne Moir and David Jessel, *Brain Sex: The Real Difference Between Men and Women* (New York: Dell Publishing, 1991), p. 45.
85. Erin Leahey and Guang Guo, "Gender Differences in Mathematical Trajectories" in *Social Forces*, Vol. 80, No. 2 (2001), pp. 713–32.
86. *Myths of Gender*, p. 31.
87. Ibid., p. 35.
88. *Sex on the Brain*, p. 58.

89. Michael S. Kimmel, "'What About the Boys?' What the Current Debates Tell Us—and Don't Tell Us—About Boys in School" in *The Gendered Society Reader*, eds. Michael S. Kimmel with Amy Aronson (Oxford: Oxford University Press, 2004), p. 253.

90. Ibid., p. 251.

91. Anne Fausto-Sterling, *Sexing the Body: Gender Politics and the Construction of Sexuality* (New York: Basic Books, 2000), p. 154.

92. Online Etymology Dictionary, http://www.etymonline.com/index.php?term=estrus

93. Robert A. Josephs, Jennifer Guinn Seller, and Matthew L. Newman, "The Mismatch Effect: When Testosterone and Status Are at Odds" in *Journal of Personality and Social Psychology*, Vol. 9, No. 6 (2006), p. 999.

94. Andrew Sullivan, "The He Hormone" in *New York Times Magazine* (April 2, 2000), http://www.nytimes.com/2000/04/02/magazine/the-he-hormone.html?pagewanted=1.

95. Ibid.

96. Ibid.

97. *Brain Sex*, p. 78.

98. *Brain Sex*, pp. 77–8.

99. "Law; Juris Cojones" in *New York Times Magazine* (November 1, 1998), http://www.nytimes.com/1998/11/01/magazine/sunday-november-1-1998-law-juris-cojones.html?pagewanted=1.

100. Ibid.

101. James M. Dabbs, Jr., "Testosterone and Occupational Achievement" in *Social Forces*, Vol. 70, No. 3 (1992), pp. 813–24.

102. Ibid., p. 819.

103. "The He Hormone." .

104. *Brain Sex*, pp. 77–8.

105. Ibid., p. 5.

106. Robert Sapolsky, "Testosterone Rules" in *The Gendered Society Reader*, p. 30.

107. Alan Booth et al., "Testosterone and Winning and Losing in Human Competition" in *Hormones and Behavior*, Vol. 23, Issue 4, (December, 1989), pp. 556–71.

108. Richard H. Rahe et al., "Psychological and Physiological Assessments on American Hostages Freed from Captivity in Iran" in *Psychosomatic Medicine* Vol. 52, Issue 1, (1990), p. 1.

109. Cited in "Testosterone and Occupational Achievement," p. 821.

110. Ibid..

111. See Adele E. Clark, *Disciplining Reproduction: Modernity, American Life Science and the Problems of Sex* (Berkeley: University of California Press, 1998), p. 126.

112. Carol M. Worthman "Hormones, Sex and Gender" in *Annual Review of Anthropology*, Vol. 24 (1995), p. 608.

113. Cited by Anne Fausto-Sterling, "The Bare Bones of Sex: Part 1—Sex and Gender" in *Signs: Journal of Women in Culture and Society*, Vol. 30, No. 2 (2005), p. 1494.

114. Ibid., p. 1515.

115. Ibid., p. 1510.

CHAPTER TWO

1. Cited in Thomas M. Laqueur, *Making Sex: The Body and Gender from the Greeks to Freud* (Cambridge MA: Harvard University Press, 1990), p. 4.

2. Ibid., p. 4.

3. Ibid., p. 35.

4. Ibid., p. 35.

5. Ibid., p. 37.

6. Ibid., p. 43.

7. Ibid., p. 124.

8. Ibid., p. 127. Also see Merry E. Wiesner, *Women and Gender in Early Modern Europe*, 2nd. ed. (Cambridge: Cambridge University Press, 2000), p. 54.

9. *Making Sex*, p. 127.

10. Ibid., p. 46.

11. Martha Bayless, *Parody in the Middle Ages: The Latin Tradition* (Ann Arbor, MI: University of Michigan Press, 1996), pp. 3–4:

    Of the skin he made him mittens,
    Made them with the fur side inside,
    Made them with the skin side outside.
    He, to get the warm side inside,
    Put the inside skin side outside.
    He, to get the cold side outside,
    Put the warm side fur side inside.
    That's why he put the fur side inside,
    Why he put the skin side outside,
    Why he turned them inside outside.

12. *Making Sex*, p. 65.

13. Ibid., p. 10.

14. See ibid., pp. 1–3.

15. Ibid., p. 116.

16. Ibid., p. 121.

17. Ibid., p. 62.

18. Ibid., p. 154.

19. Ibid., p. 197.

20. See ibid., pp. 199–200.

21. See, for example, Kathryn M. Ringrose, "Living in the Shadows: Eunuchs and Gender in Byzantium" in *Third Sex, Third Gender: Beyond Sexual Dimorphism in Culture and History*, ed. Gilbert Herdt (New York Zone Books, 1994) p. 89.

22. Lynda Coon, "Gender and the Body" in *Early Medieval Christianity, A.D. 600–1100*, Vol. 3 of the *Cambridge History of Christianity*, eds. Thomas F. X. Noble & Julia M. H. Smith (Cambridge: Cambridge University Press, 2008), pp. 433–52.

23. Alice Domurat Dreger, *Hermaphrodites and the Medical Invention of Sex* (Cambridge MA: Harvard University Press, 1998), p. 35. Actually, Laqueur does not deny that the one-sex model "lived on." See *Making Sex*, pp. 150–1.

24. *Making Sex*, p. 69.

25. Ibid., p. 16.

26. Ibid., p. 16.

27. See the Intersex Society of North America (ISNA) website at http://www.isna.org. The ISNA also uses the term *DSD* for those with disorders of sex development.

28. *Sexing the Body*, p. 35

29. *Making Sex*, p. 137.

30. Ibid., p. 140.

31. *Making Sex*, p. 138.

32. Gilbert Herdt, "Mistaken Sex: Culture, Biology and the Third Sex in New Guinea" in *Third Sex, Third Gender*, pp. 429 and 431.

33. Ibid., pp. 435–6.

34. Ibid., p. 431.

35. See *Hermaphrodites and the Medical Invention of Sex*. Also see Randolph Trumbach, "London's Sapphists: From Three Sexes to Four Genders in the Making of Modern Culture" in *Third Sex/Third Gender*, p. 112.

36. *Hermaphrodites and the Medical Invention of Sex*, p. 26.

37. Ibid., p. 85.

38. Ibid., p. 88.

39. Cited in ibid., p. 147.

40. Ibid.

41. Ibid., p. 150.

42. The Intersex Society of North American (ISNA) drew attention to these practices and asked medical professionals to end them. The ISNA recommends that intersex infants still be assigned a male or female gender at birth. See http://www.isna.org

43. *Sexing the Body*, p. 52.

44. *Hermaphrodites and the Medical Invention of Sex*, p. 39.

45. See Milton Diamond, "Sex Reassignment at Birth: Long-Term Review and Clinical Implications" in *Archives of Pediatrics and Adolescent Medicine*, Vol. 151 (1997), ttp://www.cirp.org/library/psych/diamond1/.
46. *Sexing the Body*, p. 46.
47. Suzanne J. Kessler, *Lessons from the Intersexed* (New Brunswick, NJ: Rutgers University Press, 1998), p. 25.
48. Ibid., pp. 18–9.
49. J. W. Duckett and L. S. Baskin, "Genitoplasty for Intersex Anomalies" in *European Journal of Pediatrics*, No. 152, Suppl. 2 (1993), p. 580.
50. Anne Fausto-Sterling, "How to Build a Man" in *Gender*, ed. Anna Tripp (New York: Palgrave, 2000), p. 112.
51. *Sexing the Body*, pp. 58–9.
52. *Hermaphrodites and the Medical Invention of Sex*, p. 178.
53. See, for example, *Lessons from the Intersexed*, pp. 53–64; for the Intersex Society of North America's view, see http://www.isna.org/faq/concealment
54. See http://aappolicy.aappublications.org/cgi/content/full/pediatrics;118/2/e488
55. Ibid.
56. See ibid.
57. Ibid.
58. Ibid.
59. Will Rosco, "How to Become a *Berdache*: Toward a Unified Analysis of Gender Diversity" in *Third Sex/Third Gender*, p. 330.
60. See Sabine Lang, *Men as Women, Women as Men: Changing Gender in Native American Cultures*, trans. John L. Valtine (Austin: University of Texas Press, 1998), pp. xiii–xvii.
61. "How to Become a *Berdache*," p. 335.
62. *Men as Women, Women as Men*, p. 10.
63. See ibid., p. xvii.
64. See "How to Become a *Berdache*," p. 335.
65. Ibid., p. 335.
66. Ibid., p. 355.
67. Dan Bilefsky, "Albanian Custom Fades: Women as Family Men" in *New York Times* (June 25, 2008), http://www.nytimes.com/2008/06/25/world/europe/25virgins.html?_r=1.
68. See René Grémaux, "Woman Becomes Man in the Balkans," in *Third Sex, Third Gender*, pp. 241–81, and Mildred Dickemann, "The Balkan Sworn Virgin: A Traditional European Transperson" in *Gender Blending*, eds. Bonnie Bullough, Vern L. Bullough, and James Elias (New York: Prometheus Books, 1997), pp. 248–55.
69. "The Balkan Sworn Virgin," p. 249.
70. "Woman Becomes Man in the Balkans," pp. 250 and 253.
71. "The Balkan Sworn Virgin," p. 251.

72. See "Albanian Custom Fades."
73. "Woman Becomes Man in the Balkans," p. 255.
74. "The Balkan Sworn Virgin," p. 253.
75. Serena Nanda, *Neither Man nor Woman: The Hijras of India* (Belmont, CA: Wadsworth Publishing Co., 1999).
76. Ibid., p. 15.
77. Ibid., p. 16.
78. Ibid., p. 119.
79. Serena Nanda, "Hijras as Neither Man nor Woman" in *The Lesbian and Gay Studies Reader*, eds. Henry Abelove et al. (New York: Routledge, 1993), p. 550.
80. Phyllis Randolph Frye, "The International Bill of Gender Rights vs. the Cider House Rules: Transgenders Struggle with the Courts over What Clothing They Are Allowed to Wear on the Job, Which Restroom They Are Allowed to Use on the Job, Their Right to Marry, and the Very Definition of Their Sex" in 7 *William and Mary Journal of Women and the Law* 133 (Fall 2000), p. 154.
81. Ibid., p. 156.
82. Ibid., p. 158.
83. All quotes from *Diagnostic and Statistical Manual of Mental Disorders*, 4th ed. (DSM-IV) at http://allpsych.com/disorders/dsm.html
84. "D.C. Settles Bias Suit in 1995 Death: Rescue Workers Mistreated, Mocked Injured Transvestite" in *The Washington Post* (August 11, 2000) p. B1.
85. See Alex Tresniowski, "He's Having a Baby" in *People* (April 14, 2008), p. 56.
86. Thomas Beatie, "Labor of Love" in *The Advocate* (April 8, 2008), http://www.advocate.com/article.aspx?id=22217.
87. Guy Treblay, "He's Pregnant, You're Speechless" in *New York Times* (June 22, 2008), Style Section, p. 1.
88. Thomas Beatie, Labor of Love: The Story of One Man's Extraordinary Pregnancy (Berkeley, CA: Seal Press, 2008).
89. See "Labor of Love."
90. Jeff Jacoby, "Pregnant Yes—But Not a Man" in *The Boston Globe* (April 13, 2008), http://www.boston.com/bostonglobe/editorial_opinion/oped/articles/2008/04/13/pregnant_yes___but_not_a_man.
91. Ibid. .
92. Anne Fausto-Sterling, "The Five Sexes: Why Male and Female Are Not Enough" in *The Sciences* (March/April, 1993, p. 21.
93. Melanie Blackless, Anthony Charuvastra, Amanda Derryck, Anne Fausto-Sterling, Karl Lauzanne, and Ellen Lee, "How Sexually Dimorphic Are We? Review and Synthesis" in *American Journal of Human Biology*, Vol. 12, No. 2 (2000), pp. 151–166.
94. *Transgender People and Passports*, September 2008, available at http://www.transequality.org/Resources/resources.html.

CHAPTER THREE

1. *The Second Sex*, p. 281.
2. *Man and Woman, Boy and Girl*, p. 4.
3. Harold Garfinkel, *Studies in Ethnomethodology* (Englewood Cliffs, NJ: Prentice-Hall, Inc., 1967).
4. See Edmund Husserl, *The Idea of Phenomenology*, trans. Lee Hardy (Dordrecht: Kluwer Adaemic Publishers, 1999) p. 15.
5. See Suzanne J. Kessler and Wendy McKenna, *Gender: An Ethnomethodological Approach*, (New York: John Wiley and Sons, 1978), pp. 4–5.
6. *Studies in Ethnomethodology*, p. 122.
7. Ibid., p. 119.
8. Ibid., p. 118.
9. Ibid., p. 118.
10. Ibid., p. 141.
11. Ibid., p. 146.
12. Ibid., pp. 146–7.
13. Ibid., p. 180.
14. See ibid., p. 126–7.
15. Kate Bornstein, *Gender Outlaw: On Men, Women and the Rest of Us* (New York: Vintage Press, 1995).
16. Ibid., p. 22.
17. Ibid., p. 24.
18. Ibid., p. 24.
19. *Gender: An Ethnomethodological Approach*, p. 6.
20. *Gender Outlaw*, p. 24.
21. Ibid., p. 234.
22. Ibid., p. 51.
23. Ibid., p. 22.
24. Ibid., p. 4.
25. "How to Become a *Berdache*," p. 339.
26. *Gender Outlaw*, p. 39.
27. Ibid., p. 116.
28. Ibid., p. 138.
29. Ibid., p. 136.
30. Ibid., pp. 136 and 137.
31. See Judith Butler, *Bodies that Matter: On the Discursive Limits of "Sex"* (New York: Routledge, 1993), p. 12.
32. Judith Butler, "Performative Acts and Gender Constitution: An Essay in Phenomenology and Feminist Theory" in *Theatre Journal*, Vol. 40, No. 4 (1988), p. 521.
33. Cited in Judith Butler, *Gender Trouble: Feminism and the Subversion of Identity* (New York, Routledge, 1990), p. 25.

34. Susan Marenco and Jay Mason (producers and directors), *Adventures in the Gender Trade* (videorecording) (New York: Filmakers Library, 1993).
35. *Gender Trouble*, p. 7.
36. See Luce Irigaray, "The Power of Discourse" in *This Sex Which Is Not One*, trans. Catherine Porter (Ithaca, NY: Cornell University Press, 1985), pp. 68–85.
37. Ibid., p. 78.
38. Ibid., p. 68.
39. *Gender Trouble*, p. 11.
40. Ibid.
41. Ibid.
42. *The Second Sex*, p. xxvi.
43. *Bodies that Matter*, p. 7.
44. Ibid., p. 11.
45. *Bodies that Matter*, p. 11. Cited in Sally Haslanger, "Feminism in Metaphysics: Negotiating the Natural" in *The Cambridge Companion to Feminist Philosophy*, eds. Miranda Fricker and Jennifer Hornsby (Cambridge: Cambridge University Press, 2000), p. 120.
46. "Feminism in Metaphysics," p. 121.
47. See also Linda Alcoff, *Visible Identities: Race, Gender and the Self* (Oxford: Oxford University Press, 2006), p. 170.
48. J. L. Austin, *How to Do Things with Words*, 2nd ed., ed. J. O. Urmson and Marina Sbisa (Cambridge: Harvard University Press, 1975).
49. "Performative Acts and Gender Constitution," p. 519.
50. *Bodies that Matter*, p. 13.
51. Martha Nussbaum, "The Professor of Parody: The Hip Defeatism of Judith Butler" in *The New Republic* (February 22, 1999), p. 37.
52. Ibid., p. 37.
53. Adrienne Rich, "Compulsory Heterosexuality and Lesbian Existence" in *The Lesbian and Gay Studies Reader*, eds. Henry Abelove et al. (New York: Routledge, 1993), pp. 227–254.
54. *Gender Trouble*, pp. 22–3.
55. See Michel Foucault, "Right of Death and Power over Life" in *The Foucault Reader*, ed. Paul Rabinow (New York: Pantheon Books, 1984), pp. 258–272.
56. See Michel Foucault, *The History of Sexuality*, Vol. 1, *An Introduction*, trans. Robert Hurley (New York, Vintage Books, 1998); see especially Part Two, "The Repressive Hypothesis."
57. *Bodies that Matter*, p. 9.
58. Judith Butler, "Contingent Foundations: Feminism and the Question of "Postmodernism"" in *Feminist Contentions: A Philosophical Exchange*, eds. Seyla Benhabib et al. (New York: Routledge, 1995), p. 47.
59. *Bodies that Matter*, p. 8.

60. Sue-Ellen Case, "Toward a Butch-Femme Aesthetic" in *The Lesbian and Gay Studies Reader*. See also "Womanliness as a Masquerade" in *Female Experience: Three Generations of British women Psychoanalysts on Work with Women* ed. Joan Raphael-Leff and Rozine Jozef Perelberg (London: Routldege, 1997), pp. 228–236. Butler also cites Riviere's article in *Gender Trouble*.

61. Womanliness as a Masquerade," p. 230. Cited in "Toward a Butch-Femme Aesthetic," p. 300.

62. Ibid., p. 231. Cited in "Toward a Butch-Femme Aesthetic," p. 300.

63. "Toward a Butch-Femme Aesthetic," p. 300–1.

64. Judith Butler, "The Question of Social Transformation" in *Undoing Gender* (New York: Routledge, 2004), p. 214.

65. "Toward a Butch-Femme Aesthetic," p. 305.

66. Nancy Fraser, "False Antitheses: A Response to Judith Butler and Seyla Benhabib" in *Feminist Contentions*, p. 67.

67. Ibid., p. 67.

68. Judith Butler, *The Psychic Life of Power: Theories in Subjection* (Stanford, CA: Stanford University Press, 1997), p. 14.

69. "False Antitheses," p. 68.

70. Ibid., pp. 67–68.

71. "The Professor of Parody," p. 43.

72. "False Antitheses," p. 68.

73. See ibid., p. 41.

74. Ibid., p. 41, and Seyla Benhabib, "Feminism and Postmodernism: An Uneasy Alliance," in *Feminist Contentions*, pp. 20–2.

75. Seyla Benhabib, "Subjectivity, Historiography, and Politics: Reflections on the Feminism/Postmodernism Exchange" in *Feminist Contentions*, p. 111.

76. *The Psychic Life of Power*, p. 109.

77. "The Question of Social Transformation," p. 206.

78. Ibid., p. 224.

79. Ibid., p. 225.

80. *Bodies that Matter*, p. 8.

81. "The Professor of Parody," p. 45.

82. "The Question of Social Transformation," p. 221.

CHAPTER FOUR

1. Sally Haslanger, "Gender and Race: (What) Are They? (What) Do We Want Them to Be" in *Nous*, Vol. 34, No. 1 (2000), p. 37.

2. The Combahee River Collective, "A Black Feminist Statement" in *The Second Wave: A Reader in Feminist Theory*, ed. Linda Nicholson (New York:

Routledge, 1997), p. 69. Also see *This Bridge Called My Back: Writings by Radical Women of Color*, eds. Cherríe Maraga and Gloria Anzaldúa (New York: Kitchen Table: Women of Color Press, 1983).

3. See Aída Hurtado, "Relating to Privilege: Seduction and Rejection in the Subordination of White Women and Women of Color" in *Signs: Journal of Women in Culture and Society*, Vol. 14, No. 4 (1989), pp. 849–50.

4. Kimberle Crenshaw, "Mapping the Margins: Intersectionality, Identity Politics and Violence Against Women of Color," *Stanford Law Review* Vol. 43, No. 6 (July 1993), p. 1252–3.

5. Ibid., p. 1258. See also Beth E. Richie, "A Black Feminist Reflection on the Antiviolence Movement" in *Signs: Journal of Women in Culture and Society*, Vol. 25, No. 4. (2000), p. 1134.

6. Gary Lafree, Rape and Criminal Justice: the social Construction of Sexual Assault (New York: Wadsworth Publishing Company, 1989).

7. Ibid., p. 1277.

8. Ibid., pp. 1277–8.

9. Ibid., p. 1262.

10. Ibid., p. 1263.

11. bell hooks, *Ain't I a Woman: Black Women and Feminism* (Boston: South End Press, 1981), p. 7.

12. *All the Women Are White, All the Blacks Are Men, but Some of Us Are Brave*, eds. Gloria T. Hull, Patricia Bell Scott, and Barbara Smith (Old Westbury, NY: Feminist Press, 1982).

13. "A Black Feminist Reflection on the Antiviolence Movement," p. 1135.

14. Natalie J. Sokoloff and Ida Dupont, "Domestic Violence at the Intersections of Race, Class, and Gender" in *Violence Against Women*, Vol. 11, No. 1 (2005), p. 41.

15. Trinh T. Minh, *Woman, Native, Other: Writing Postcoloniality and Feminism* (Bloomington: University of Indiana Press, 1989), p. 82.

16. Chandra Talpade Mohanty, *Feminism Without Borders: Decolonizing Theory, Practicing Solidarity* (Durham, NC: Duke University Press, 2003), p. 23.

17. Ibid., p. 242.

18. Ibid., p. 240.

19. *The Second Sex*, p. xlviii.

20. See Elizabeth V. Spelman, *Inessential Woman: Problems of Exclusion in Feminist Thought* (Boston: Beacon Press, 1988).

21. *The Second Sex*, p. l.

22. "Relating to Privilege," p. 844.

23. August Bebel, *Woman under Socialism* (1891), 33rd ed., trans. Daniel De Leon (New York: Source Book Press, 1970).

24. *The Second Sex*, p. liii.

25. *Inessential Woman*, p. 65.

26. Judith Oakley, "Rereading *The Second Sex*" in Elizabeth Fallaize (ed.) *Simone de Beauvoir: A Critical Reader* (New York: Routledge, 1998.) p. 21.
27. *Inessential Woman*, p. 65.
28. Toril Moi, "'Independent Women' and 'Narratives of Liberation'" in *Simone de Beauvoir: A Critical Reader*, p. 91, n.16.
29. Nancy Chodorow, *The Reproduction of Mothering: Psychoanalysis and the Sociology of Gender* (Berkeley: University of California Press, 1978; new preface, 1999).
30. Ibid., p. 83.
31. See above, Chapter One, note 30.
32. Ibid., p. 96.
33. Ibid., p. 129.
34. Ibid., p. 169.
35. Carol Gilligan, *In a Different Voice: Psychological Theory and Women's Development* (Cambridge, MA: Harvard University Press, 1982), p. 8.
36. Sigmund Freud, "Some Psychical Consequences of the Anatomical Distinction between the Sexes" (1925) in *The Standard Edition of the Complete Psychological Works of Sigmund Freud*, Vol. 19 (1923–1925) (London: Hogarth Press), pp. 257–8. See *In a Different Voice*, p. 7.
37. See *In a Different Voice*, p. 18.
38. Lawrence Kohlberg, The Philosophy of Moral Development: Moral Stages and The Idea of Justice (New York: Harper and Rowe, 1981) p. 18.
39. Ibid.
40. Lawrence Kohlberg, "The Claim to Moral Adequacy of a Highest Stage of Moral Judgment" in *The Journal of Philosophy*, Vol. 70, No. 18, (1973), p. 631.
41. See *In a Different Voice*, especially pp. 20–9.
42. Patricia Hill Collins, "The Social Construction of Black Feminist Thought" in *Signs: Journal of Women in Culture and Society*, Vol. 14, No. 4 (1989), p. 751.
43. Ibid., p. 184.
44. Judith Lorber, "On the Reproduction of Motherhood: A Methodological Debate" in *Signs: Journal of Women in Culture and Society*, Vol. 6, No. 3 (1981), p. 483.
45. See Denise A. Segura and Jennifer L. Pierce, "Chicana/o Family Structure and Gender Personality: Chodorow, Familism, and Psychoanalytic Sociology Revisited" in *Signs: Journal of Women in Culture and Society* Vol. 19, No. 1 (1993), p. 62.
46. Oyeronke Oyewumi, "Family Bonds/Conceptual Binds: African Notes on Feminist Epistemologies" in *Signs: Journal of Women in Culture and Society*, Vol. 25. No. 4, (2000)p. 1097.
47. Chodorow, "Preface to the Second Edition" in *The Reproduction of Mothering*, pp. xi–xii.

48. See *In a Different Voice*, p. 2.

49. John Gray, Men Are from Mars, Women Are from Venus: The Classic Guide to Understanding the Opposite Sex (New York: Harper Paperbacks, 2004).

50. Nancy Fraser and Linda J. Nicholson, "Social Criticism without Philosophy: An Encounter between Feminism and Postmodernism" in *Feminism/Postmodernism*, ed. Linda J. Nicholson (New York: Routledge, 1990.)

51. See, for example: Evelynn M. Hammonds, "Toward a Genealogy of Black Female Sexuality: The Problematic of Silence" in *Feminist Theory and the Body: A Reader*, eds. Janet Price and Margaret Shildrick. (New York: Routledge, 1997), pp. 249–59 and Chandra Talpade Mohanty, "Women Workers and Capitalist Scripts: Ideologies of Domination, Common Interests and the Politics of Solidarity" in *Feminist Genealogies, Colonial Legacies, Democratic Futures*, eds. M. Jacqui Alexander and Chandra Talpade Mohanty, (New York: Routledge, 1997) , pp. 3–29 and the two special issues of *Hypatia: A Journal of Feminist Philosophy* on *Feminism and Disability*: Part I, Vol. 16, No. 4 (2001) and Part II, Vol. 17, No. 3 (2002).

52. Leslie McCall, "The Complexity of Intersectionality" in *Signs: Journal of Women in Culture and Society*, Vol. 30, No. 3 (2005), pp. 1771–1800.

53. Susan Gubar, "What Ails Feminist Criticism" in *Critical Inquiry*, Vo. 24, No. 4 (1998), p. 901.

54. See Christine Di Stefano, "Dilemmas of Difference: Feminism, Modernity, and Postmodernism"; Susan Bordo, "Feminism, Postmodernism, and Gender-Skepticism"; and Nancy Hartsock, "Foucault on Power: A Theory for Women?" in *Feminism/Postmodernism* (New York: Routledge, 1990), pp. 62–82, pp. 113–56, and pp. 157–75, respectively.

55. Iris Marion Young, "Gender as Seriality: Thinking about Women as a Social Collective" in *Signs: Journal of Women in Culture and Society*, Vol. 19, No. 3 (1994), p. 719.

56. "Gender as Seriality," p. 724.

57. Ibid., p. 725.

58. Ibid., p. 737.

59. See ibid., p. 737.

60. "Gender and Race," p. 38.

61. Ibid., p. 42.

62. Iris Marion Young, "*Justice and the Politics of Difference* (Princeton, NJ: Princeton University Press, 1990), p. 41. Cited in "Gender and Race," p. 40.

63. "Gender and Race," p. 50.

64. Julia Kristeva, "Woman Can Never be Defined" in *New French Feminisms*, eds. Elaine Marks and Isabelle de Courtivron (New York: Schocken Books, 1981), p. 137.

65. Joan W. Scott, "Work Identities for Men and Women: The Politics of Work and Family in the Parisian Garment Trades in 1848" in *Gender*

and the Politics of History (New York: Columbia University Press, 1988), pp. 93–112.

66. Ibid., p. 97.
67. Ibid., p. 112.
68. Denise Riley, *Am I That Name? Feminism and the Category of "Women" in History* (Minneapolis: University of Minnesota Press, 1988), p. 113.
69. *Equal Employment Opportunity Commission v. Sears, Roebuck and Co.* (628 F. Supp. 1264.) See Scott, "The Sears Case" in *Gender and the Politics of History*, pp. 167–77. I also talk briefly about Scott's analysis of this case in *After Identity*, p. 159.
70. See "Orders of Proof," reprinted in Jacquelyn Dowd Hall and Sandi E. Cooper, "Women's History Goes to Trial: *EEOC v. Sears, Roebuck and Company*" in *Signs: Journal of Women in Culture and Society,* Vol. 11, No. 4 (1986), p. 761.
71. Ibid., p. 771.
72. *Am I That Name*, p. 113.
73. Ibid., pp. 113–4.
74. Ibid., p. 112.
75. In "Social Criticism without Philosophy."
76. Ibid., p. 34.
77. Ibid., p. 35.
78. Ibid., p. 34–5.
79. Ibid., p. 35.
80. *Feminism Without Borders*, p. 242,
81. Ibid.

CHAPTER FIVE

1. Hans-Georg Gadamer *Truth and Method* (1960), 2nd ed., trans. rev. by Joel Weinsheimer and Donald Marshall (New York: Continuum Publishing Company, 1994).
2. *Visible Identities*, p. 95.
3. Ibid., p. 96.
4. Ibid.
5. Ibid. p. 52.
6. Ibid.,p. 96. .
7. Ibid., p. 98.
8. Ibid..
9. *Truth and Method*, p. 401.
10. Ibid., p. 102.
11. Ibid., p. 106.
12. Ibid., p. 107.
13. Ibid., p. 176.

14. Ibid., p. 126.
15. Emily Martin, *The Woman in the Body: A Cultural Analysis of Reproduction*, rev. ed. (Boston: Beacon Press, 2001), pp. xi–xii.
16. Ibid., p. xii.
17. Ibid., p. xii.
18. Jeffrey T. Nealon, "The Discipline of Deconstruction" in *PMLA*, Vol. 107, No. 5 (1992), pp. 1266–79.
19. *Truth and Method*, p. 294.
20. Mary A. Favret, "Free and Happy: Jane Austen in America" in *Janeites: Austen's Disciples and Devotees*, ed. Deidre Lynch (Princeton, NJ: Princeton University Press, 2000).
21. Eve Kosofsky Sedgwick, "Jane Austen and the Masturbating Girl" in *Critical Inquiry*, Vol. 17, No. 4 (1991).
22. Claudia L. Johnson, *Jane Austen: Women, Politics and the Novel* (Chicago: University of Chicago Press, 1988).
23. *Truth and Method*, p. 296.
24. George Haggerty, "Fanny Price: 'Is She Solemn?—Is She Queer?—Is She Prudish?': An Essay in Memory of Ralph W. Rader" in *The Eighteenth Century: Theory and Interpretation* (forthcoming).
25. Londa Schiebinger, "Skeletons in the Closet: The First Illustrations of the Female Skeleton in Eighteenth-Century Anatomy" in *Representations*, No. 14 (1986), pp. 42–82.
26. Defense of Marriage Act, Pub. L. No. 104–109, § 2(a), 110 Stat.2419 (1996) (codified as amended at 28 U.S.C.A. § 1738C (West Supp.1997)
27. I also take up this question in *After Identity* Chapter 6..
28. William M. Hohengarten, "Same-Sex Marriage and the Right of Privacy" in *The Yale Law Journal*, Vol. 103, No. 6 (1994), pp. 1495–31.
29. Ibid., p. 1499.
30. Letter from United States General Accounting Office, Office of the General Counsel to The Honorable Henry J. Hyde Chairman, Committee on the Judiciary, House of Representatives (www.gao.gov/archive/1997/og97016.pdf).
31. 543 N.E. 2d 49 (N.Y. 1989); quoted in "Same-Sex Marriage and the Right of Privacy," pp. 1503–4.
32. Ibid., p. 1504.
33. *Perez v. Sharp* (32 Cal 2d 711), p. 715.
34. *Loving v. Virginia* (388 U.S. 1), p. 12.
35. *Turner v. Safley*, 482 U. S. 78 (1987).
36. *Zablocki v. Redhail*, 434 U.S. 374 (1978).
37. See, for example, Dwight D. Duncan, "The Federal Marriage Amendment and Rule by Judges" in *Harvard Journal of Law and Public Policy*, Vol. 27 (Spring 2004);Teresa Stanton Collett, "Recognizing Same-Sex Marriage: Asking for the Impossible?" in *The Catholic University Law Review*, Vol. 47

(Summer 1998), pp. 1262–3, and both David Organ Coolidge and George Dent at "The University of Chicago Law School Roundtable" (7 *University of Chicago Law School Roundtable* (2000)), pp. 41 and 47.

38. *Hernandez v. Robles*, Lexis pagination, p. 8.
39. "The University of Chicago Law School Roundtable," p. 47.
40. In *Re Marriage of Sterling Simmons and Jennifer Simmons* (355 Ill. App. 3d 942).
41. Ibid.
42. *Littleton v. Prange* (9 S.W. 3d 223; Tex App.).
43. Ibid. at 226.
44. Ibid.
45. Ibid. at 230.
46. Ibid.
47. Cited in Jennifer Finney Boylan, "Is My Marriage Gay?" in *New York Times* (May 12, 2009), p. A27.

CHAPTER SIX

1. For example, see *Myths of Gender* and *Sexing the Body*.
2. See, for example, Elisabeth Carlsen et al., "Evidence for decreasing quality of semen over past 50 years," in *British Medical Journal*, Vol. 305 (September 1992), pp 609–13.
3. For example, see *Gender Trouble*.

Index